# TEACHER'S PET PUBLICATIONS

PUZZLE PACK
for
Fahrenheit 451
based on the book by
Ray Bradbury

Written by
William T. Collins

© 2005 Teacher's Pet Publications
All Rights Reserved

The materials in this packet are copyrighted
by Teacher's Pet Publications, Inc.

These pages may be duplicated by the purchaser
for use in the purchaser's own classroom.

Copying any of these materials and distributing them
for any other purpose is a violation of the copyright laws.

© 2005 Teacher's Pet Publications, Inc.
www.tpet.com

INTRODUCTION
If you already own the LitPlan for this title, this Puzzle Pack will refresh your Unit Resource Materials and Vocabulary Resource Materials sections plus give you additional materials you can substitute into the tests. If you do not already have a complete LitPlan, these pages will give you some supplemental materials to use with your own plan. There are two main groups of materials: one set for unit words (such as characters' names, symbols, places, etc.) and one set for vocabulary words associated with the book.

WORD LIST
There is a word list for both the unit words and the vocabulary words. These lists show you which words are being used in the materials and the clues or definitions being used for those words. You may want to give students a word list with clues/definitions to help them, or you may want students to only have a word list (without clues/definitions) if you want them to work a little harder. Both are available for duplication. The word lists can also be your "calling key" for the bingo games.

FILL IN THE BLANK AND MATCHING
There are 4 each of the fill in the blank and matching worksheets for both the unit and vocabulary words. These pages can be used either as extra worksheets for students or as objective parts of a unit test. They can be done individually if students need extra help or as a whole class activity to review the material covered.

MAGIC SQUARES
The magic squares not only reinforce the material covered but also work on reasoning and math skills. Many teachers have told us that their students really enjoy doing these!

WORD SEARCH PUZZLES
The word search words go in all directions, as indicated on your answer keys. Two of the word search puzzles have the clues listed rather than the words. This makes the puzzle a little more difficult, but it reinforces the material better. Two word search puzzles have words only for students who find the clue puzzles too difficult.

CROSSWORD PUZZLES
Both unit and vocabulary word sections have 4 crossword puzzles.

BINGO CARDS
There are 32 individual bingo cards for the unit words and 32 individual bingo cards for the vocabulary words. You can use your word list as a "call list," calling the words at random and marking them off of your list as you go, or you could use the flash cards by cutting them apart and drawing the words at random from a hat (or box or whatever). To make a better review, you might ask for the definition and spelling of each word as you call it out—or you could call out the definitions and have students tell you the words they need to look for on the puzzle.

JUGGLE LETTERS
The vocabulary juggle letter game is intended to help students learn the spellings of the words. One sheet has the definitions listed on it as an extra help for students who need it or to reinforce the definitions if you choose to do so.

FLASH CARDS
We've included a set of vocabulary flash cards you can duplicate, cut, and fold for your students. Some teachers make a few sets for general use by the class; others make a set for each student. Some teachers duplicate them for each student and have the students cut & fold their own. You can cut out just the words and put them in a hat, have each student pick out one word and write the definition and a sentence for that word. Students then swap words and papers, with the next student adding a sentence of his own under the last one. You can have students swap as many times as you like. Each time the student will read the sentences written prior to his own and then add a sentence. You can cut out the words and definitions separately and play "I Have; Who Has?" Each student in the room draws a word and definition. The first student says, "I have (the name of the word). Who has the definition?" The student with the definition reads it then says, "I have (the name of the vocabulary word she has). Who has the definition?" The round continues until all words and definitions have been given.

Fahrenheit 451 Word List

No	Word	Clue/Definition
1.	ASHES	Remains after burning
2.	ATTACK	Montag was afraid the hounds would do this
3.	ATTIC	Montag took a book from the old lady's ___.
4.	BEATTY	Captain of the firemen
5.	BEETLES	Transportation
6.	BOMB	One blew up the city
7.	BOOKS	Montag & Faber were going to plant these in firemen's houses
8.	BRADBURY	Author
9.	BURN	Destroy with flames
10.	CACOPHONY	Harsh-sounding words
11.	CAR	Clarisse was hit & killed by one
12.	CLARISSE	She liked to think and talk
13.	DIE	Stop living
14.	DIGEST	Condensed version of a book
15.	EAR	Place where radio transmitter was put for use
16.	ECCLESIASTES	Book Montag memorized
17.	ESCAPE	To get away
18.	FABER	He helped Montag
19.	FAHRENHEIT	_____ 451
20.	FIRE	Flames
21.	FIREMEN	They burned books & started fires
22.	FREE	Not bound
23.	GRILLE	Place Montag first hid his books
24.	HELMET	Fireman's head protector
25.	HOBOS	They memorized literature.
26.	HOUND	Mechanical ___; chased criminals
27.	IGNITER	Flame starter
28.	INCINERATOR	Montag burned a book of poetry in one.
29.	INFORMANTS	People who told fireman who had books
30.	KEROSENE	It smelled like perfume to Montag
31.	MECHANICAL	_____ Hound
32.	MILDRED	Wife; informer; attempted suicide
33.	MONTAG	He snatched books & hid them & got in trouble
34.	NIGHT	Time when most fires were set
35.	PARK	Place where Montag met Faber
36.	PARLORWALLS	Mildred's pastime; huge television
37.	PHOENIX	Rising from the ashes
38.	PILLS	Mildred took an overdose of sleeping ___.
39.	RADIO	Small communications device used by Montag & Faber
40.	READ	What we do with books
41.	RIVER	Where Montag went after fleeing Faber's house
42.	SEASHELLS	Ear thimbles
43.	LOUIS	St. ____;Faber's destination
44.	TRACKS	Montag's path to safety
45.	WINE	Rain tasted like this beverage
46.	YARD	Montag hid his books there after the ladies left.

Fahrenheit 451 Fill In The Blank 1

_____ 1. She liked to think and talk

_____ 2. Flames

_____ 3. Montag hid his books there after the ladies left.

_____ 4. They memorized literature.

_____ 5. Montag & Faber were going to plant these in firemen's houses

_____ 6. Flame starter

_____ 7. Wife; informer; attempted suicide

_____ 8. Montag burned a book of poetry in one.

_____ 9. Transportation

_____ 10. Book Montag memorized

_____ 11. People who told fireman who had books

_____ 12. Remains after burning

_____ 13. Place Montag first hid his books

_____ 14. Stop living

_____ 15. Place where radio transmitter was put for use

_____ 16. ____ Hound

_____ 17. Mechanical ___; chased criminals

_____ 18. To get away

_____ 19. Destroy with flames

_____ 20. Small communications device used by Montag & Faber

Fahrenheit 451 Fill In The Blank 1 Answer Key

CLARISSE	1. She liked to think and talk
FIRE	2. Flames
YARD	3. Montag hid his books there after the ladies left.
HOBOS	4. They memorized literature.
BOOKS	5. Montag & Faber were going to plant these in firemen's houses
IGNITER	6. Flame starter
MILDRED	7. Wife; informer; attempted suicide
INCINERATOR	8. Montag burned a book of poetry in one.
BEETLES	9. Transportation
ECCLESIASTES	10. Book Montag memorized
INFORMANTS	11. People who told fireman who had books
ASHES	12. Remains after burning
GRILLE	13. Place Montag first hid his books
DIE	14. Stop living
EAR	15. Place where radio transmitter was put for use
MECHANICAL	16. ____ Hound
HOUND	17. Mechanical ___; chased criminals
ESCAPE	18. To get away
BURN	19. Destroy with flames
RADIO	20. Small communications device used by Montag & Faber

Fahrenheit 451 Fill In The Blank 2

_____ 1. Clarisse was hit & killed by one

_____ 2. Ear thimbles

_____ 3. They memorized literature.

_____ 4. Rising from the ashes

_____ 5. Small communications device used by Montag & Faber

_____ 6. Transportation

_____ 7. Destroy with flames

_____ 8. It smelled like perfume to Montag

_____ 9. Rain tasted like this beverage

_____ 10. Montag burned a book of poetry in one.

_____ 11. Place Montag first hid his books

_____ 12. He helped Montag

_____ 13. They burned books & started fires

_____ 14. Time when most fires were set

_____ 15. Harsh-sounding words

_____ 16. Captain of the firemen

_____ 17. Author

_____ 18. She liked to think and talk

_____ 19. Mechanical ___; chased criminals

_____ 20. One blew up the city

Fahrenheit 451 Fill In The Blank 2 Answer Key

CAR	1. Clarisse was hit & killed by one
SEASHELLS	2. Ear thimbles
HOBOS	3. They memorized literature.
PHOENIX	4. Rising from the ashes
RADIO	5. Small communications device used by Montag & Faber
BEETLES	6. Transportation
BURN	7. Destroy with flames
KEROSENE	8. It smelled like perfume to Montag
WINE	9. Rain tasted like this beverage
INCINERATOR	10. Montag burned a book of poetry in one.
GRILLE	11. Place Montag first hid his books
FABER	12. He helped Montag
FIREMEN	13. They burned books & started fires
NIGHT	14. Time when most fires were set
CACOPHONY	15. Harsh-sounding words
BEATTY	16. Captain of the firemen
BRADBURY	17. Author
CLARISSE	18. She liked to think and talk
HOUND	19. Mechanical ___; chased criminals
BOMB	20. One blew up the city

Fahrenheit 451 Fill In The Blank 3

_____ 1. Montag took a book from the old lady's ___.

_____ 2. Stop living

_____ 3. Small communications device used by Montag & Faber

_____ 4. Captain of the firemen

_____ 5. Mechanical ___; chased criminals

_____ 6. Place Montag first hid his books

_____ 7. What we do with books

_____ 8. Flames

_____ 9. Montag hid his books there after the ladies left.

_____ 10. They burned books & started fires

_____ 11. Ear thimbles

_____ 12. Mildred took an overdose of sleeping ___.

_____ 13. Remains after burning

_____ 14. Clarisse was hit & killed by one

_____ 15. Time when most fires were set

_____ 16. ____ Hound

_____ 17. Place where radio transmitter was put for use

_____ 18. St.____;Faber's destination

_____ 19. Where Montag went after fleeing Faber's house

_____ 20. She liked to think and talk

Fahrenheit 451 Fill In The Blank 3 Answer Key

ATTIC	1. Montag took a book from the old lady's ___.
DIE	2. Stop living
RADIO	3. Small communications device used by Montag & Faber
BEATTY	4. Captain of the firemen
HOUND	5. Mechanical ___; chased criminals
GRILLE	6. Place Montag first hid his books
READ	7. What we do with books
FIRE	8. Flames
YARD	9. Montag hid his books there after the ladies left.
FIREMEN	10. They burned books & started fires
SEASHELLS	11. Ear thimbles
PILLS	12. Mildred took an overdose of sleeping ___.
ASHES	13. Remains after burning
CAR	14. Clarisse was hit & killed by one
NIGHT	15. Time when most fires were set
MECHANICAL	16. ____ Hound
EAR	17. Place where radio transmitter was put for use
LOUIS	18. St. ____;Faber's destination
RIVER	19. Where Montag went after fleeing Faber's house
CLARISSE	20. She liked to think and talk

Fahrenheit 451 Fill In The Blank 4

_____ 1. Montag took a book from the old lady's ___.
_____ 2. _____ 451
_____ 3. One blew up the city
_____ 4. Captain of the firemen
_____ 5. Montag was afraid the hounds would do this
_____ 6. Rising from the ashes
_____ 7. Where Montag went after fleeing Faber's house
_____ 8. He helped Montag
_____ 9. People who told fireman who had books
_____ 10. Small communications device used by Montag & Faber
_____ 11. Author
_____ 12. It smelled like perfume to Montag
_____ 13. Book Montag memorized
_____ 14. Time when most fires were set
_____ 15. St._____;Faber's destination
_____ 16. Mildred's pastime; huge television
_____ 17. He snatched books & hid them & got in trouble
_____ 18. Clarisse was hit & killed by one
_____ 19. Montag burned a book of poetry in one.
_____ 20. _____ Hound

Fahrenheit 451 Fill In The Blank 4 Answer Key

ATTIC	1. Montag took a book from the old lady's ___.
FAHRENHEIT	2. _____ 451
BOMB	3. One blew up the city
BEATTY	4. Captain of the firemen
ATTACK	5. Montag was afraid the hounds would do this
PHOENIX	6. Rising from the ashes
RIVER	7. Where Montag went after fleeing Faber's house
FABER	8. He helped Montag
INFORMANTS	9. People who told fireman who had books
RADIO	10. Small communications device used by Montag & Faber
BRADBURY	11. Author
KEROSENE	12. It smelled like perfume to Montag
ECCLESIASTES	13. Book Montag memorized
NIGHT	14. Time when most fires were set
LOUIS	15. St.____;Faber's destination
PARLORWALLS	16. Mildred's pastime; huge television
MONTAG	17. He snatched books & hid them & got in trouble
CAR	18. Clarisse was hit & killed by one
INCINERATOR	19. Montag burned a book of poetry in one.
MECHANICAL	20. ____ Hound

Fahrenheit 451 Matching 1

___ 1. HOUND   A. Montag was afraid the hounds would do this
___ 2. WINE   B. Mildred took an overdose of sleeping ___.
___ 3. MILDRED   C. What we do with books
___ 4. HELMET   D. Rising from the ashes
___ 5. RADIO   E. Montag's path to safety
___ 6. ATTACK   F. Montag & Faber were going to plant these in firemen's houses
___ 7. PARLORWALLS   G. Mildred's pastime; huge television
___ 8. ESCAPE   H. Ear thimbles
___ 9. CLARISSE   I. Captain of the firemen
___10. BOOKS   J. Rain tasted like this beverage
___11. IGNITER   K. Time when most fires were set
___12. PARK   L. Fireman's head protector
___13. NIGHT   M. Transportation
___14. KEROSENE   N. Flame starter
___15. READ   O. To get away
___16. TRACKS   P. Mechanical ___; chased criminals
___17. BEATTY   Q. She liked to think and talk
___18. SEASHELLS   R. Place where radio transmitter was put for use
___19. GRILLE   S. It smelled like perfume to Montag
___20. BEETLES   T. Place where Montag met Faber
___21. PHOENIX   U. People who told fireman who had books
___22. INFORMANTS   V. Montag hid his books there after the ladies left.
___23. EAR   W. Wife; informer; attempted suicide
___24. PILLS   X. Small communications device used by Montag & Faber
___25. YARD   Y. Place Montag first hid his books

Fahrenheit 451 Matching 1 Answer Key

P - 1. HOUND	A.	Montag was afraid the hounds would do this
J - 2. WINE	B.	Mildred took an overdose of sleeping ___.
W - 3. MILDRED	C.	What we do with books
L - 4. HELMET	D.	Rising from the ashes
X - 5. RADIO	E.	Montag's path to safety
A - 6. ATTACK	F.	Montag & Faber were going to plant these in firemen's houses
G - 7. PARLORWALLS	G.	Mildred's pastime; huge television
O - 8. ESCAPE	H.	Ear thimbles
Q - 9. CLARISSE	I.	Captain of the firemen
F - 10. BOOKS	J.	Rain tasted like this beverage
N - 11. IGNITER	K.	Time when most fires were set
T - 12. PARK	L.	Fireman's head protector
K - 13. NIGHT	M.	Transportation
S - 14. KEROSENE	N.	Flame starter
C - 15. READ	O.	To get away
E - 16. TRACKS	P.	Mechanical ___; chased criminals
I - 17. BEATTY	Q.	She liked to think and talk
H - 18. SEASHELLS	R.	Place where radio transmitter was put for use
Y - 19. GRILLE	S.	It smelled like perfume to Montag
M - 20. BEETLES	T.	Place where Montag met Faber
D - 21. PHOENIX	U.	People who told fireman who had books
U - 22. INFORMANTS	V.	Montag hid his books there after the ladies left.
R - 23. EAR	W.	Wife; informer; attempted suicide
B - 24. PILLS	X.	Small communications device used by Montag & Faber
V - 25. YARD	Y.	Place Montag first hid his books

Fahrenheit 451 Matching 2

___ 1. DIGEST   A. Condensed version of a book
___ 2. MECHANICAL   B. Rain tasted like this beverage
___ 3. FAHRENHEIT   C. Captain of the firemen
___ 4. BURN   D. Rising from the ashes
___ 5. FIRE   E. Mildred's pastime; huge television
___ 6. YARD   F. Montag took a book from the old lady's ___.
___ 7. CACOPHONY   G. ____ Hound
___ 8. DIE   H. Time when most fires were set
___ 9. PHOENIX   I. Wife; informer; attempted suicide
___10. GRILLE   J. Montag's path to safety
___11. LOUIS   K. Where Montag went after fleeing Faber's house
___12. BEATTY   L. Mildred took an overdose of sleeping ___.
___13. WINE   M. Destroy with flames
___14. PARLORWALLS   N. Author
___15. PILLS   O. Flames
___16. ATTIC   P. Montag hid his books there after the ladies left.
___17. SEASHELLS   Q. Stop living
___18. RIVER   R. Ear thimbles
___19. TRACKS   S. St.____;Faber's destination
___20. BOMB   T. One blew up the city
___21. MILDRED   U. Fireman's head protector
___22. BRADBURY   V. Place Montag first hid his books
___23. HELMET   W. Mechanical ___; chased criminals
___24. NIGHT   X. Harsh-sounding words
___25. HOUND   Y. ____ 451

Fahrenheit 451 Matching 2 Answer Key

A - 1. DIGEST	A.	Condensed version of a book
G - 2. MECHANICAL	B.	Rain tasted like this beverage
Y - 3. FAHRENHEIT	C.	Captain of the firemen
M - 4. BURN	D.	Rising from the ashes
O - 5. FIRE	E.	Mildred's pastime; huge television
P - 6. YARD	F.	Montag took a book from the old lady's ___.
X - 7. CACOPHONY	G.	___ Hound
Q - 8. DIE	H.	Time when most fires were set
D - 9. PHOENIX	I.	Wife; informer; attempted suicide
V - 10. GRILLE	J.	Montag's path to safety
S - 11. LOUIS	K.	Where Montag went after fleeing Faber's house
C - 12. BEATTY	L.	Mildred took an overdose of sleeping ___.
B - 13. WINE	M.	Destroy with flames
E - 14. PARLORWALLS	N.	Author
L - 15. PILLS	O.	Flames
F - 16. ATTIC	P.	Montag hid his books there after the ladies left.
R - 17. SEASHELLS	Q.	Stop living
K - 18. RIVER	R.	Ear thimbles
J - 19. TRACKS	S.	St.___;Faber's destination
T - 20. BOMB	T.	One blew up the city
I - 21. MILDRED	U.	Fireman's head protector
N - 22. BRADBURY	V.	Place Montag first hid his books
U - 23. HELMET	W.	Mechanical ___; chased criminals
H - 24. NIGHT	X.	Harsh-sounding words
W - 25. HOUND	Y.	___ 451

Fahrenheit 451 Matching 3

___ 1. CAR   A. He snatched books & hid them & got in trouble
___ 2. MONTAG   B. Flame starter
___ 3. FIRE   C. Montag burned a book of poetry in one.
___ 4. LOUIS   D. Not bound
___ 5. FABER   E. Rain tasted like this beverage
___ 6. BOMB   F. Captain of the firemen
___ 7. READ   G. St.____;Faber's destination
___ 8. WINE   H. Destroy with flames
___ 9. BEATTY   I. One blew up the city
___10. TRACKS   J. Mechanical ___; chased criminals
___11. IGNITER   K. Montag & Faber were going to plant these in firemen's houses
___12. HOUND   L. Author
___13. PARLORWALLS   M. _____ 451
___14. FREE   N. He helped Montag
___15. BOOKS   O. Where Montag went after fleeing Faber's house
___16. FAHRENHEIT   P. Montag was afraid the hounds would do this
___17. INCINERATOR   Q. Place Montag first hid his books
___18. BURN   R. Flames
___19. DIE   S. Montag's path to safety
___20. ATTACK   T. Stop living
___21. GRILLE   U. Fireman's head protector
___22. HELMET   V. Mildred's pastime; huge television
___23. BRADBURY   W. Montag took a book from the old lady's ___.
___24. ATTIC   X. What we do with books
___25. RIVER   Y. Clarisse was hit & killed by one

Fahrenheit 451 Matching 3 Answer Key

- Y - 1. CAR
- A - 2. MONTAG
- R - 3. FIRE
- G - 4. LOUIS
- N - 5. FABER
- I - 6. BOMB
- X - 7. READ
- E - 8. WINE
- F - 9. BEATTY
- S - 10. TRACKS
- B - 11. IGNITER
- J - 12. HOUND
- V - 13. PARLORWALLS
- D - 14. FREE
- K - 15. BOOKS
- M - 16. FAHRENHEIT
- C - 17. INCINERATOR
- H - 18. BURN
- T - 19. DIE
- P - 20. ATTACK
- Q - 21. GRILLE
- U - 22. HELMET
- L - 23. BRADBURY
- W - 24. ATTIC
- O - 25. RIVER

A. He snatched books & hid them & got in trouble
B. Flame starter
C. Montag burned a book of poetry in one.
D. Not bound
E. Rain tasted like this beverage
F. Captain of the firemen
G. St.____;Faber's destination
H. Destroy with flames
I. One blew up the city
J. Mechanical ___; chased criminals
K. Montag & Faber were going to plant these in firemen's houses
L. Author
M. _____ 451
N. He helped Montag
O. Where Montag went after fleeing Faber's house
P. Montag was afraid the hounds would do this
Q. Place Montag first hid his books
R. Flames
S. Montag's path to safety
T. Stop living
U. Fireman's head protector
V. Mildred's pastime; huge television
W. Montag took a book from the old lady's ___.
X. What we do with books
Y. Clarisse was hit & killed by one

Fahrenheit 451 Matching 4

___ 1. INCINERATOR A. St.____; Faber's destination
___ 2. BOMB B. Captain of the firemen
___ 3. IGNITER C. Small communications device used by Montag & Faber
___ 4. BEETLES D. ____ Hound
___ 5. BOOKS E. Place where Montag met Faber
___ 6. PARK F. To get away
___ 7. ASHES G. It smelled like perfume to Montag
___ 8. HOBOS H. He helped Montag
___ 9. PILLS I. Montag hid his books there after the ladies left.
___10. ESCAPE J. Montag & Faber were going to plant these in firemen's houses
___11. LOUIS K. They memorized literature.
___12. RADIO L. Flames
___13. BEATTY M. He snatched books & hid them & got in trouble
___14. YARD N. Ear thimbles
___15. SEASHELLS O. Not bound
___16. KEROSENE P. Remains after burning
___17. TRACKS Q. Montag burned a book of poetry in one.
___18. FIRE R. _____ 451
___19. MONTAG S. Flame starter
___20. BRADBURY T. Mildred took an overdose of sleeping ___.
___21. FABER U. Author
___22. MECHANICAL V. Transportation
___23. WINE W. One blew up the city
___24. FAHRENHEIT X. Rain tasted like this beverage
___25. FREE Y. Montag's path to safety

Fahrenheit 451 Matching 4 Answer Key

Q - 1. INCINERATOR	A.	St.____ ;Faber's destination
W - 2. BOMB	B.	Captain of the firemen
S - 3. IGNITER	C.	Small communications device used by Montag & Faber
V - 4. BEETLES	D.	____ Hound
J - 5. BOOKS	E.	Place where Montag met Faber
E - 6. PARK	F.	To get away
P - 7. ASHES	G.	It smelled like perfume to Montag
K - 8. HOBOS	H.	He helped Montag
T - 9. PILLS	I.	Montag hid his books there after the ladies left.
F - 10. ESCAPE	J.	Montag & Faber were going to plant these in firemen's houses
A - 11. LOUIS	K.	They memorized literature.
C - 12. RADIO	L.	Flames
B - 13. BEATTY	M.	He snatched books & hid them & got in trouble
I - 14. YARD	N.	Ear thimbles
N - 15. SEASHELLS	O.	Not bound
G - 16. KEROSENE	P.	Remains after burning
Y - 17. TRACKS	Q.	Montag burned a book of poetry in one.
L - 18. FIRE	R.	_____ 451
M - 19. MONTAG	S.	Flame starter
U - 20. BRADBURY	T.	Mildred took an overdose of sleeping ___.
H - 21. FABER	U.	Author
D - 22. MECHANICAL	V.	Transportation
X - 23. WINE	W.	One blew up the city
R - 24. FAHRENHEIT	X.	Rain tasted like this beverage
O - 25. FREE	Y.	Montag's path to safety

Copyrighted

Fahrenheit 451 Magic Squares 1

Match the definition with the vocabulary word. Put your answers in the magic squares below. When your answers are correct, all columns and rows will add to the same number.

A. NIGHT   E. LOUIS   I. YARD   M. PHOENIX
B. CACOPHONY   F. GRILLE   J. MILDRED   N. ASHES
C. HOBOS   G. DIGEST   K. HELMET   O. TRACKS
D. READ   H. BEETLES   L. FAHRENHEIT   P. PARLORWALLS

1. Place Montag first hid his books
2. Montag hid his books there after the ladies left.
3. Montag's path to safety
4. What we do with books
5. Rising from the ashes
6. Harsh-sounding words
7. Transportation
8. Fireman's head protector
9. They memorized literature.
10. Mildred's pastime; huge television
11. Wife; informer; attempted suicide
12. St.____;Faber's destination
13. _____ 451
14. Condensed version of a book
15. Time when most fires were set
16. Remains after burning

A=	B=	C=	D=
E=	F=	G=	H=
I=	J=	K=	L=
M=	N=	O=	P=

Fahrenheit 451 Magic Squares 1 Answer Key

Match the definition with the vocabulary word. Put your answers in the magic squares below. When your answers are correct, all columns and rows will add to the same number.

A. NIGHT
B. CACOPHONY
C. HOBOS
D. READ
E. LOUIS
F. GRILLE
G. DIGEST
H. BEETLES
I. YARD
J. MILDRED
K. HELMET
L. FAHRENHEIT
M. PHOENIX
N. ASHES
O. TRACKS
P. PARLORWALLS

1. Place Montag first hid his books
2. Montag hid his books there after the ladies left.
3. Montag's path to safety
4. What we do with books
5. Rising from the ashes
6. Harsh-sounding words
7. Transportation
8. Fireman's head protector
9. They memorized literature.
10. Mildred's pastime; huge television
11. Wife; informer; attempted suicide
12. St.____;Faber's destination
13. _____ 451
14. Condensed version of a book
15. Time when most fires were set
16. Remains after burning

A=15	B=6	C=9	D=4
E=12	F=1	G=14	H=7
I=2	J=11	K=8	L=13
M=5	N=16	O=3	P=10

Fahrenheit 451 Magic Squares 2

Match the definition with the vocabulary word. Put your answers in the magic squares below. When your answers are correct, all columns and rows will add to the same number.

A. BOOKS
B. HOUND
C. FAHRENHEIT
D. NIGHT
E. SEASHELLS
F. IGNITER
G. ECCLESIASTES
H. HOBOS
I. PHOENIX
J. MECHANICAL
K. FIRE
L. KEROSENE
M. INFORMANTS
N. BURN
O. INCINERATOR
P. PARK

1. Destroy with flames
2. Book Montag memorized
3. It smelled like perfume to Montag
4. Montag & Faber were going to plant these in firemen's houses
5. Flames
6. Mechanical ___; chased criminals
7. People who told fireman who had books
8. They memorized literature.
9. Ear thimbles
10. Place where Montag met Faber
11. _____ 451
12. ____ Hound
13. Time when most fires were set
14. Rising from the ashes
15. Flame starter
16. Montag burned a book of poetry in one.

A=	B=	C=	D=
E=	F=	G=	H=
I=	J=	K=	L=
M=	N=	O=	P=

Fahrenheit 451 Magic Squares 2 Answer Key

Match the definition with the vocabulary word. Put your answers in the magic squares below. When your answers are correct, all columns and rows will add to the same number.

A. BOOKS   E. SEASHELLS   I. PHOENIX   M. INFORMANTS
B. HOUND   F. IGNITER   J. MECHANICAL   N. BURN
C. FAHRENHEIT   G. ECCLESIASTES K. FIRE   O. INCINERATOR
D. NIGHT   H. HOBOS   L. KEROSENE   P. PARK

1. Destroy with flames
2. Book Montag memorized
3. It smelled like perfume to Montag
4. Montag & Faber were going to plant these in firemen's houses
5. Flames
6. Mechanical ___; chased criminals
7. People who told fireman who had books
8. They memorized literature.
9. Ear thimbles
10. Place where Montag met Faber
11. _____ 451
12. ____ Hound
13. Time when most fires were set
14. Rising from the ashes
15. Flame starter
16. Montag burned a book of poetry in one.

A=4	B=6	C=11	D=13
E=9	F=15	G=2	H=8
I=14	J=12	K=5	L=3
M=7	N=1	O=16	P=10

Fahrenheit 451 Magic Squares 3

Match the definition with the vocabulary word. Put your answers in the magic squares below. When your answers are correct, all columns and rows will add to the same number.

A. CACOPHONY E. CLARISSE   I. HOBOS   M. FIREMEN
B. INCINERATOR F. PARLORWALLS J. ATTIC   N. KEROSENE
C. FREE   G. PARK   K. ASHES   O. SEASHELLS
D. BEETLES   H. TRACKS   L. PILLS   P. EAR

1. Montag's path to safety
2. Harsh-sounding words
3. Montag burned a book of poetry in one.
4. Place where Montag met Faber
5. Montag took a book from the old lady's ___.
6. Ear thimbles
7. Place where radio transmitter was put for use
8. They memorized literature.
9. Remains after burning
10. It smelled like perfume to Montag
11. They burned books & started fires
12. Mildred took an overdose of sleeping ___.
13. She liked to think and talk
14. Transportation
15. Not bound
16. Mildred's pastime; huge television

A=	B=	C=	D=
E=	F=	G=	H=
I=	J=	K=	L=
M=	N=	O=	P=

Fahrenheit 451 Magic Squares 3 Answer Key

Match the definition with the vocabulary word. Put your answers in the magic squares below. When your answers are correct, all columns and rows will add to the same number.

A. CACOPHONY
B. INCINERATOR
C. FREE
D. BEETLES
E. CLARISSE
F. PARLORWALLS
G. PARK
H. TRACKS
I. HOBOS
J. ATTIC
K. ASHES
L. PILLS
M. FIREMEN
N. KEROSENE
O. SEASHELLS
P. EAR

1. Montag's path to safety
2. Harsh-sounding words
3. Montag burned a book of poetry in one.
4. Place where Montag met Faber
5. Montag took a book from the old lady's ___.
6. Ear thimbles
7. Place where radio transmitter was put for use
8. They memorized literature.
9. Remains after burning
10. It smelled like perfume to Montag
11. They burned books & started fires
12. Mildred took an overdose of sleeping ___.
13. She liked to think and talk
14. Transportation
15. Not bound
16. Mildred's pastime; huge television

A=2	B=3	C=15	D=14
E=13	F=16	G=4	H=1
I=8	J=5	K=9	L=12
M=11	N=10	O=6	P=7

Fahrenheit 451 Magic Squares 4

Match the definition with the vocabulary word. Put your answers in the magic squares below. When your answers are correct, all columns and rows will add to the same number.

A. MONTAG
B. BOMB
C. ATTIC
D. BEATTY
E. PILLS
F. IGNITER
G. INFORMANTS
H. FAHRENHEIT
I. ATTACK
J. CLARISSE
K. BOOKS
L. HELMET
M. ESCAPE
N. RADIO
O. FIREMEN
P. PARK

1. To get away
2. Flame starter
3. _____ 451
4. They burned books & started fires
5. Fireman's head protector
6. Montag took a book from the old lady's ____.
7. He snatched books & hid them & got in trouble
8. She liked to think and talk
9. Montag & Faber were going to plant these in firemen's houses
10. Captain of the firemen
11. One blew up the city
12. Montag was afraid the hounds would do this
13. Small communications device used by Montag & Faber
14. Mildred took an overdose of sleeping ____.
15. People who told fireman who had books
16. Place where Montag met Faber

A=	B=	C=	D=
E=	F=	G=	H=
I=	J=	K=	L=
M=	N=	O=	P=

Fahrenheit 451 Magic Squares 4 Answer Key

Match the definition with the vocabulary word. Put your answers in the magic squares below. When your answers are correct, all columns and rows will add to the same number.

A. MONTAG   E. PILLS   I. ATTACK   M. ESCAPE
B. BOMB   F. IGNITER   J. CLARISSE   N. RADIO
C. ATTIC   G. INFORMANTS   K. BOOKS   O. FIREMEN
D. BEATTY   H. FAHRENHEIT   L. HELMET   P. PARK

1. To get away
2. Flame starter
3. _____ 451
4. They burned books & started fires
5. Fireman's head protector
6. Montag took a book from the old lady's ___.
7. He snatched books & hid them & got in trouble
8. She liked to think and talk
9. Montag & Faber were going to plant these in firemen's houses
10. Captain of the firemen
11. One blew up the city
12. Montag was afraid the hounds would do this
13. Small communications device used by Montag & Faber
14. Mildred took an overdose of sleeping ___.
15. People who told fireman who had books
16. Place where Montag met Faber

A=7	B=11	C=6	D=10
E=14	F=2	G=15	H=3
I=12	J=8	K=9	L=5
M=1	N=13	O=4	P=16

Fahrenheit 451 Word Search 1

```
K I G N I T E R S X T C A C O P H O N Y
H E G M T J Y M T I X G R F C K D Z Z P
L E R R L R G X E S M H R N W V G B D S
F K L O Z J A H S E T S A I S E L C C E
J R J M S F N C D W F D T W L W Z P Q J
D T F D E E S J K S E A S H E L L S J Q
X N Z Q R T N C Z S T C E C D B E D L K
I M R H P R G E D Y N H G H T O Q N Z S
N P A R L O R W A L L S I L O M L U G C
F F M X C R Q F Y R U B D A R B O O K S
O M P I B P M Q M H X A S Q S D O H R F
R M T L E C S H L Y E W L C E S X S J V
M T Q N S S J B T R E N L R S L M S F Z
A S H E S T L O U I S X I N E O H P S N
N F R M I R F Y D R K F P G N Z B E W E
T A I E R V S S A Z N T E T H E L C P F
S B V R A F R E E R K R A P A T T A C K
F E E I L C P D N G D G R T E F C R D D
N R R F C M W R I C R Q T E Z S J F B H
R A D I O K T L W M V Y B D E R D L I M
```

Author (8)
Book Montag memorized (12)
Captain of the firemen (6)
Clarisse was hit & killed by one (3)
Condensed version of a book (6)
Destroy with flames (4)
Ear thimbles (9)
St.____;Faber's destination (7)
Fireman's head protector (6)
Flame starter (7)
Flames (4)
Harsh-sounding words (9)
He helped Montag (5)
He snatched books & hid them & got in trouble (6)
It smelled like perfume to Montag (8)
Mechanical ___; chased criminals (5)
Mildred took an overdose of sleeping ___. (5)
Mildred's pastime; huge television (11)
Montag & Faber were going to plant these in firemen's houses (5)
Montag hid his books there after the ladies left. (4)
Montag took a book from the old lady's ___. (5)
Montag was afraid the hounds would do this (6)
Montag's path to safety (6)
Not bound (4)
One blew up the city (4)
People who told fireman who had books (10)
Place Montag first hid his books (6)
Place where Montag met Faber (4)
Place where radio transmitter was put for use (3)
Rain tasted like this beverage (4)
Remains after burning (5)
Rising from the ashes (7)
She liked to think and talk (8)
Small communications device used by Montag & Faber (5)
Stop living (3)
They burned books & started fires (7)
They memorized literature. (5)
Time when most fires were set (5)
To get away (6)
Transportation (7)
What we do with books (4)
Where Montag went after fleeing Faber's house (5)
Wife; informer; attempted suicide (7)
_____ 451 (10)

Fahrenheit 451 Word Search 1 Answer Key

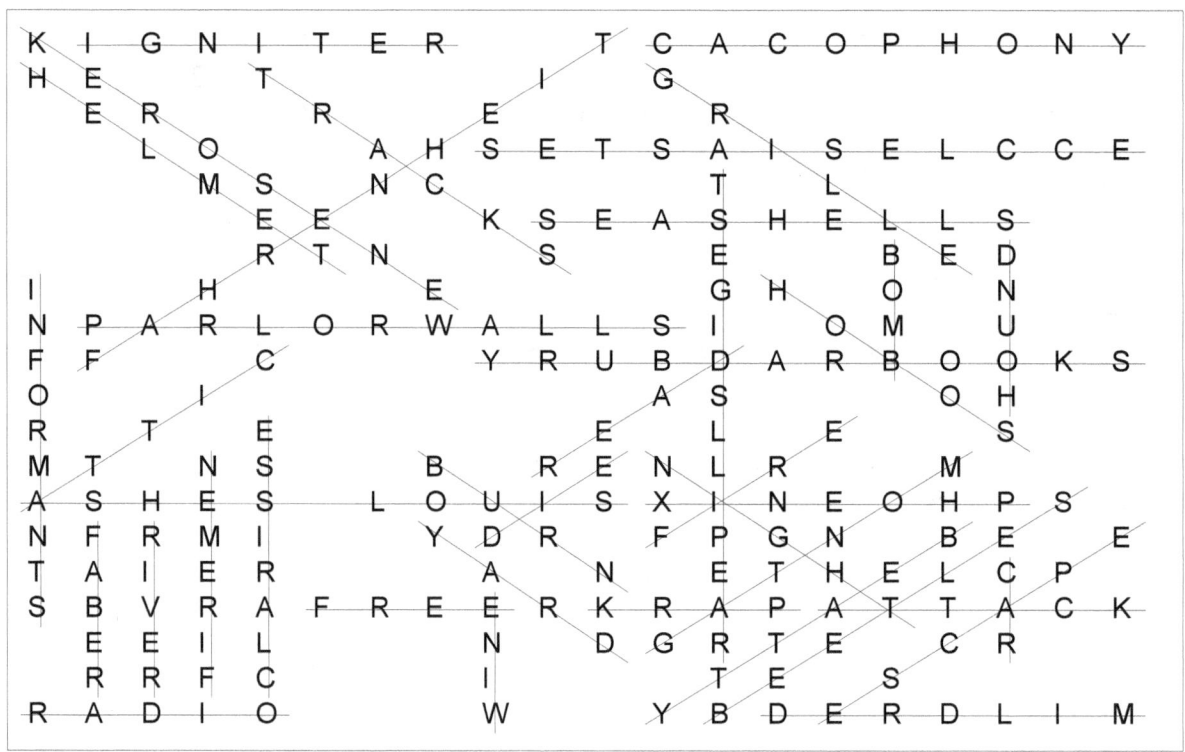

Author (8)
Book Montag memorized (12)
Captain of the firemen (6)
Clarisse was hit & killed by one (3)
Condensed version of a book (6)
Destroy with flames (4)
Ear thimbles (9)
St.____;Faber's destination (7)
Fireman's head protector (6)
Flame starter (7)
Flames (4)
Harsh-sounding words (9)
He helped Montag (5)
He snatched books & hid them & got in trouble (6)
It smelled like perfume to Montag (8)
Mechanical ___; chased criminals (5)
Mildred took an overdose of sleeping ___. (5)
Mildred's pastime; huge television (11)
Montag & Faber were going to plant these in firemen's houses (5)
Montag hid his books there after the ladies left. (4)
Montag took a book from the old lady's ___. (5)
Montag was afraid the hounds would do this (6)
Montag's path to safety (6)
Not bound (4)
One blew up the city (4)
People who told fireman who had books (10)
Place Montag first hid his books (6)
Place where Montag met Faber (4)
Place where radio transmitter was put for use (3)
Rain tasted like this beverage (4)
Remains after burning (5)
Rising from the ashes (7)
She liked to think and talk (8)
Small communications device used by Montag & Faber (5)
Stop living (3)
They burned books & started fires (7)
They memorized literature. (5)
Time when most fires were set (5)
To get away (6)
Transportation (7)
What we do with books (4)
Where Montag went after fleeing Faber's house (5)
Wife; informer; attempted suicide (7)
_____ 451 (10)

Fahrenheit 451 Word Search 2

```
I Y G V S P H O E N I X G R R P I L L S
N R T G D E Z C E C C L E S I A S T E S
C L A C I N A H C E M B Z Q V J T H L X
I L R Z Y M N S D T A N N X E J Q V S H
N I G H T X Q P H F S K C A R T Y M T E
E L S T N T W R R E E S C A P E N I L M
R K D B H Q R E N B L Z G F F C B L O S
A X D Z H R B T P V S L N R G I I D U R
T M V Y S S S I E A D H S E S R R R I C
O F I R E M E N Q Z S T S E G I D E S W
R R M D N Z E G Z L Z H B K A H L D N X
N A E M R S L I L G Z B E E V R Y S X M
H D D A O F P A C G C O S S E Q S R R Y
E I R R D N W G A T N O M L E T P A R K
L O E T Z R F T R T B K L I N F L U Z Q
M K Z H O R T Y M O T S D P I N B E H L
E D C L G A R N H D X I B M W D D N S F
T H R Y C L A R I S S E C O A D R A Y H
F A G K C A C O P H O N Y R M U S Q V S
P B E A T T Y H O U N D B K B B V L Y J
```

Author (8)
Book Montag memorized (12)
Captain of the firemen (6)
Clarisse was hit & killed by one (3)
Condensed version of a book (6)
Destroy with flames (4)
Ear thimbles (9)
St.____;Faber's destination (7)
Fireman's head protector (6)
Flame starter (7)
Flames (4)
Harsh-sounding words (9)
He helped Montag (5)
He snatched books & hid them & got in trouble (6)
It smelled like perfume to Montag (8)
Mechanical ___; chased criminals (5)
Mildred took an overdose of sleeping ___. (5)
Mildred's pastime; huge television (11)
Montag & Faber were going to plant these in firemen's houses (5)
Montag burned a book of poetry in one. (11)
Montag hid his books there after the ladies left. (4)
Montag took a book from the old lady's ___. (5)

Montag was afraid the hounds would do this (6)
Montag's path to safety (6)
Not bound (4)
One blew up the city (4)
Place Montag first hid his books (6)
Place where Montag met Faber (4)
Place where radio transmitter was put for use (3)
Rain tasted like this beverage (4)
Remains after burning (5)
Rising from the ashes (7)
She liked to think and talk (8)
Small communications device used by Montag & Faber (5)
Stop living (3)
They burned books & started fires (7)
They memorized literature. (5)
Time when most fires were set (5)
To get away (6)
Transportation (7)
What we do with books (4)
Where Montag went after fleeing Faber's house (5)
Wife; informer; attempted suicide (7)
____ Hound (10)

Fahrenheit 451 Word Search 2 Answer Key

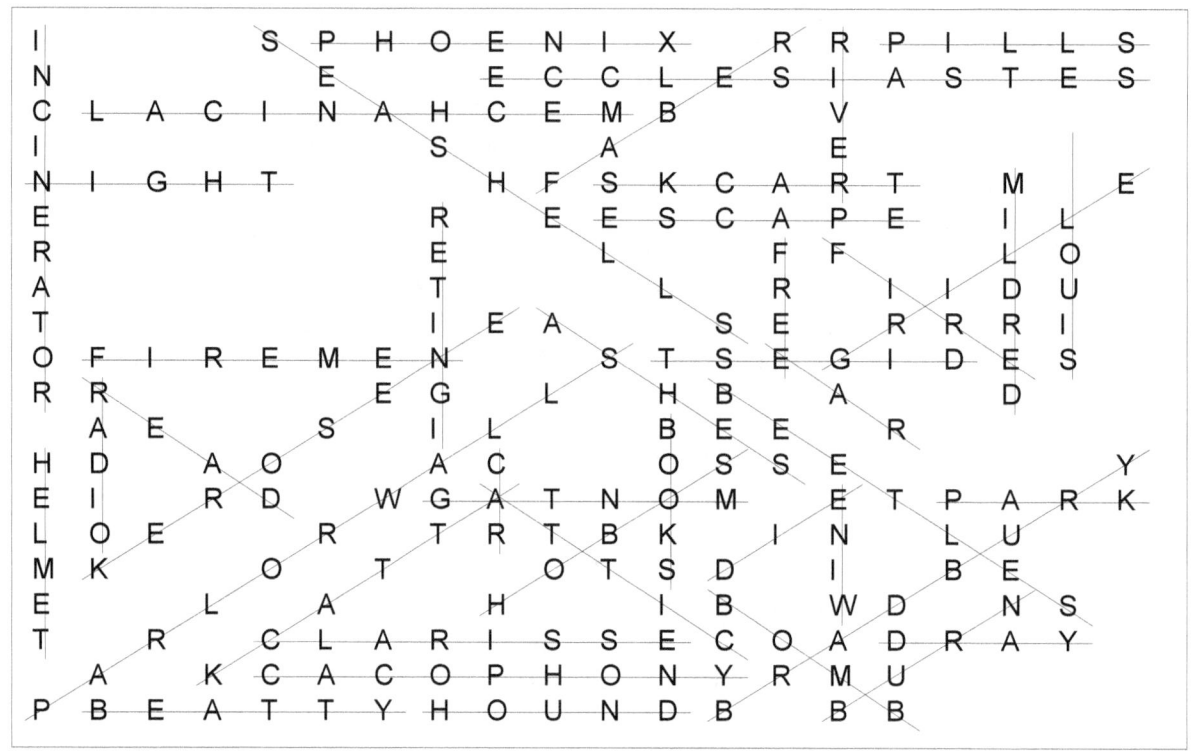

Author (8)
Book Montag memorized (12)
Captain of the firemen (6)
Clarisse was hit & killed by one (3)
Condensed version of a book (6)
Destroy with flames (4)
Ear thimbles (9)
St.____; Faber's destination (7)
Fireman's head protector (6)
Flame starter (7)
Flames (4)
Harsh-sounding words (9)
He helped Montag (5)
He snatched books & hid them & got in trouble (6)
It smelled like perfume to Montag (8)
Mechanical ___; chased criminals (5)
Mildred took an overdose of sleeping ___. (5)
Mildred's pastime; huge television (11)
Montag & Faber were going to plant these in firemen's houses (5)
Montag burned a book of poetry in one. (11)
Montag hid his books there after the ladies left. (4)
Montag took a book from the old lady's ___. (5)
Montag was afraid the hounds would do this (6)
Montag's path to safety (6)
Not bound (4)
One blew up the city (4)
Place Montag first hid his books (6)
Place where Montag met Faber (4)
Place where radio transmitter was put for use (3)
Rain tasted like this beverage (4)
Remains after burning (5)
Rising from the ashes (7)
She liked to think and talk (8)
Small communications device used by Montag & Faber (5)
Stop living (3)
They burned books & started fires (7)
They memorized literature. (5)
Time when most fires were set (5)
To get away (6)
Transportation (7)
What we do with books (4)
Where Montag went after fleeing Faber's house (5)
Wife; informer; attempted suicide (7)
____ Hound (10)

Fahrenheit 451 Word Search 3

```
I N F O R M A N T S W D I C W W R L F T
P J Q H O R F V P F R J Q G N R E V I R
L B R I G H E S C A H L R S N I F E R R
Y R D K B K D A Z H R I T A D I H B E V
X A S H E S H L D C L L F W T N T R D Q
R D R L A S V V F L O R O A E T A E E T
Z B Z D T T C V E U S J D R B C I T R D
K U J D T G N A I J Z W H Y W E Y C D V
B R H F Y W F S P K C A T T A A R S L W
W Y O E V K I L C E F N R T B Y L E I G
H C U K L S J N W A R A M Z O M S L M K
P L N F E M E H E U C T B M O B X T S W
J A D D R R E A B K H O D Q K R S E O X
H R R J Y E O T S G C X P S S E D E B R
V I C K S Y E S I H W V E H G Z T B O T
D S L X S M X N E C E T Q I O E A R H H
W S T L D I T G L N S L D B L N L T Z X
B E L R N P N B L A E L L Y T X Y T V Y
F I B E D E X F I K G M F S N L F M F R
P R O W M G P S M E C H A N I C A L S H
S H D E A X E Z J Z T V J M B N Q L Q C
P S R T P L P D K F M G W N R F F V J J
P I N S C H R K J X C B Y Y F Q Q L X Y
F O R C I N C I N E R A T O R Q W S H R
M Y E P T Q Z G J W Z Q J Y P W F Y X T
```

ASHES	CAR	FIREMEN	MECHANICAL	RIVER
ATTACK	CLARISSE	FREE	MILDRED	SEASHELLS
ATTIC	DIE	GRILLE	MONTAG	LOUIS
BEATTY	DIGEST	HELMET	NIGHT	TRACKS
BEETLES	EAR	HOBOS	PARK	WINE
BOMB	ECCLESIASTES	HOUND	PARLORWALLS	YARD
BOOKS	ESCAPE	IGNITER	PHOENIX	
BRADBURY	FABER	INCINERATOR	PILLS	
BURN	FAHRENHEIT	INFORMANTS	RADIO	
CACOPHONY	FIRE	KEROSENE	READ	

Fahrenheit 451 Word Search 3 Answer Key

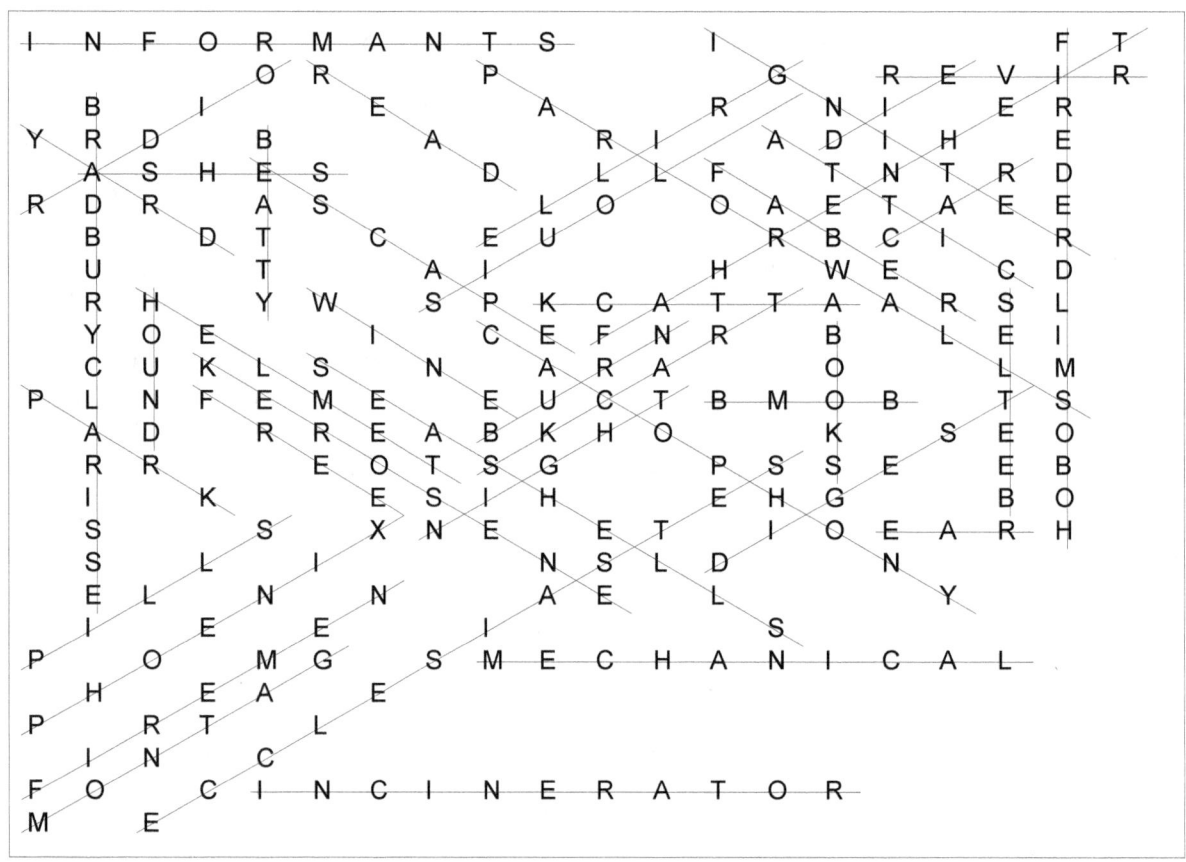

ASHES	CAR	FIREMEN	MECHANICAL	RIVER
ATTACK	CLARISSE	FREE	MILDRED	SEASHELLS
ATTIC	DIE	GRILLE	MONTAG	LOUIS
BEATTY	DIGEST	HELMET	NIGHT	TRACKS
BEETLES	EAR	HOBOS	PARK	WINE
BOMB	ECCLESIASTES	HOUND	PARLORWALLS	YARD
BOOKS	ESCAPE	IGNITER	PHOENIX	
BRADBURY	FABER	INCINERATOR	PILLS	
BURN	FAHRENHEIT	INFORMANTS	RADIO	
CACOPHONY	FIRE	KEROSENE	READ	

Fahrenheit 451 Word Search 4

```
C T G R J W R C M E C H A N I C A L Z D
W W B W Y B O N R K W P J P J Y B J D S
M Q T S C F T W N P J V Z F Q K X Z L V
S W Q E S K A W D Z R Z C J P P Q N T T
C R Z T V R R N P R K Q B S H T D Y M T
V T C S W F E X L T G B D T S B D W F R
S N F A J T N T V G R D T E K L O K S A
S D V I S Q I I A D E B G Y V P Z O C C
T N H S J I C T G V A I U A A R S S K K
F I R E M E N C K H D H G R I L L E D S
B J I L L O I F L R T F L D N L A N I E
B D Y C M M F X O A P O C F I R U U R V
V X V C R C E G D R R A A P H O O I S Z
M H S E H S A T G W M I R M H L F R E E
D I V C F S D C A L I A S K T B A A A N
S I L Q A S R L O D L N N S R O B D S P
R B W D H S L A B P T P E T E M E I H D
X E B Z R S P T E B H H K B S B R O E T
G E R H E E V T A I V O Z E N F B R L Y
K T A Q N A D I T H G E N K R O M V L Z
X L D N H J T C T G D N S Y S O J S S R
Q E B B E T Q T Y K B I I C M G S G P C
H S U K I V Z Q A K B X N T A J Q E B J
R H R F T Z N B C C G N P P E P Y C N Q
M B Y B V K B W M K K Q M C C R E J S E
```

ASHES	CAR	FIREMEN	MECHANICAL	RIVER
ATTACK	CLARISSE	FREE	MILDRED	SEASHELLS
ATTIC	DIE	GRILLE	MONTAG	LOUIS
BEATTY	DIGEST	HELMET	NIGHT	TRACKS
BEETLES	EAR	HOBOS	PARK	WINE
BOMB	ECCLESIASTES	HOUND	PARLORWALLS	YARD
BOOKS	ESCAPE	IGNITER	PHOENIX	
BRADBURY	FABER	INCINERATOR	PILLS	
BURN	FAHRENHEIT	INFORMANTS	RADIO	
CACOPHONY	FIRE	KEROSENE	READ	

Fahrenheit 451 Word Search 4 Answer Key

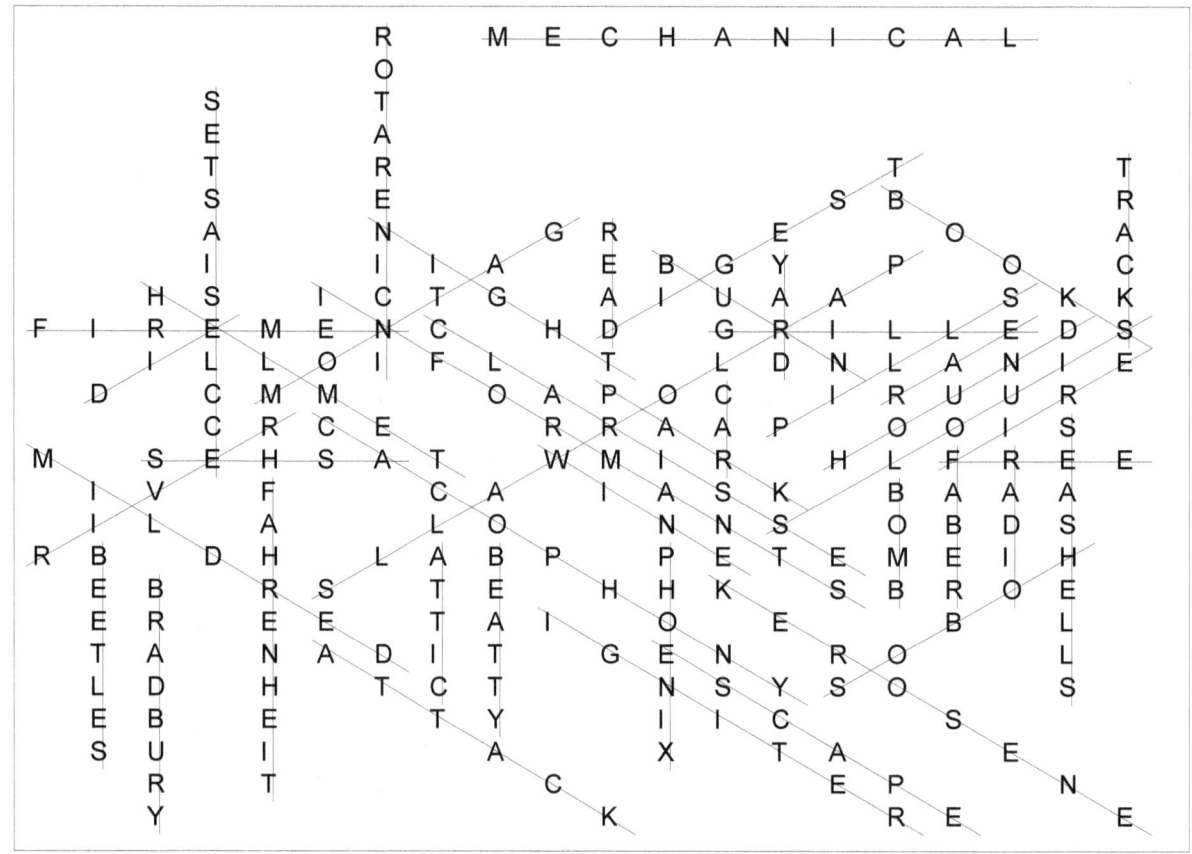

ASHES	CAR	FIREMEN	MECHANICAL	RIVER
ATTACK	CLARISSE	FREE	MILDRED	SEASHELLS
ATTIC	DIE	GRILLE	MONTAG	LOUIS
BEATTY	DIGEST	HELMET	NIGHT	TRACKS
BEETLES	EAR	HOBOS	PARK	WINE
BOMB	ECCLESIASTES	HOUND	PARLORWALLS	YARD
BOOKS	ESCAPE	IGNITER	PHOENIX	
BRADBURY	FABER	INCINERATOR	PILLS	
BURN	FAHRENHEIT	INFORMANTS	RADIO	
CACOPHONY	FIRE	KEROSENE	READ	

Fahrenheit 451 Crossword 1

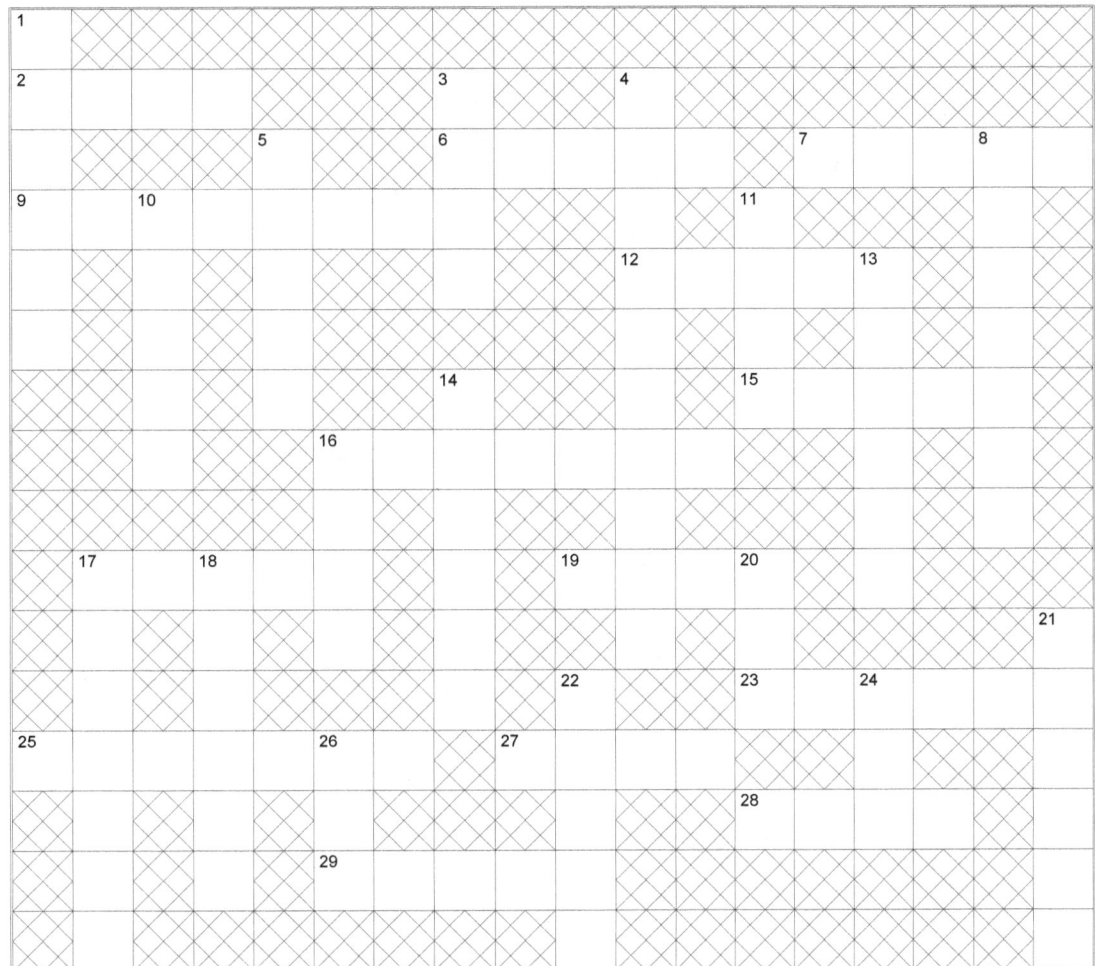

Across
2. What we do with books
6. Where Montag went after fleeing Faber's house
7. Montag took a book from the old lady's ___.
9. She liked to think and talk
12. Mechanical ___; chased criminals
15. Time when most fires were set
16. Rising from the ashes
17. He helped Montag
19. Montag hid his books there after the ladies left.
23. To get away
25. Transportation
27. One blew up the city
28. Flames
29. Small communications device used by Montag & Faber

Down
1. Montag's path to safety
3. Not bound
4. ___ Hound
5. Mildred took an overdose of sleeping ___.
8. Flame starter
10. Remains after burning
11. Destroy with flames
13. Condensed version of a book
14. He snatched books & hid them & got in trouble
16. Place where Montag met Faber
17. They burned books & started fires
18. Captain of the firemen
20. Stop living
21. Fireman's head protector
22. They memorized literature.
24. Clarisse was hit & killed by one
26. Place where radio transmitter was put for use

Fahrenheit 451 Crossword 1 Answer Key

Across
2. What we do with books
6. Where Montag went after fleeing Faber's house
7. Montag took a book from the old lady's ___.
9. She liked to think and talk
12. Mechanical ___; chased criminals
15. Time when most fires were set
16. Rising from the ashes
17. He helped Montag
19. Montag hid his books there after the ladies left.
23. To get away
25. Transportation
27. One blew up the city
28. Flames
29. Small communications device used by Montag & Faber

Down
1. Montag's path to safety
3. Not bound
4. ___ Hound
5. Mildred took an overdose of sleeping ___.
8. Flame starter
10. Remains after burning
11. Destroy with flames
13. Condensed version of a book
14. He snatched books & hid them & got in trouble
16. Place where Montag met Faber
17. They burned books & started fires
18. Captain of the firemen
20. Stop living
21. Fireman's head protector
22. They memorized literature.
24. Clarisse was hit & killed by one
26. Place where radio transmitter was put for use

Fahrenheit 451 Crossword 2

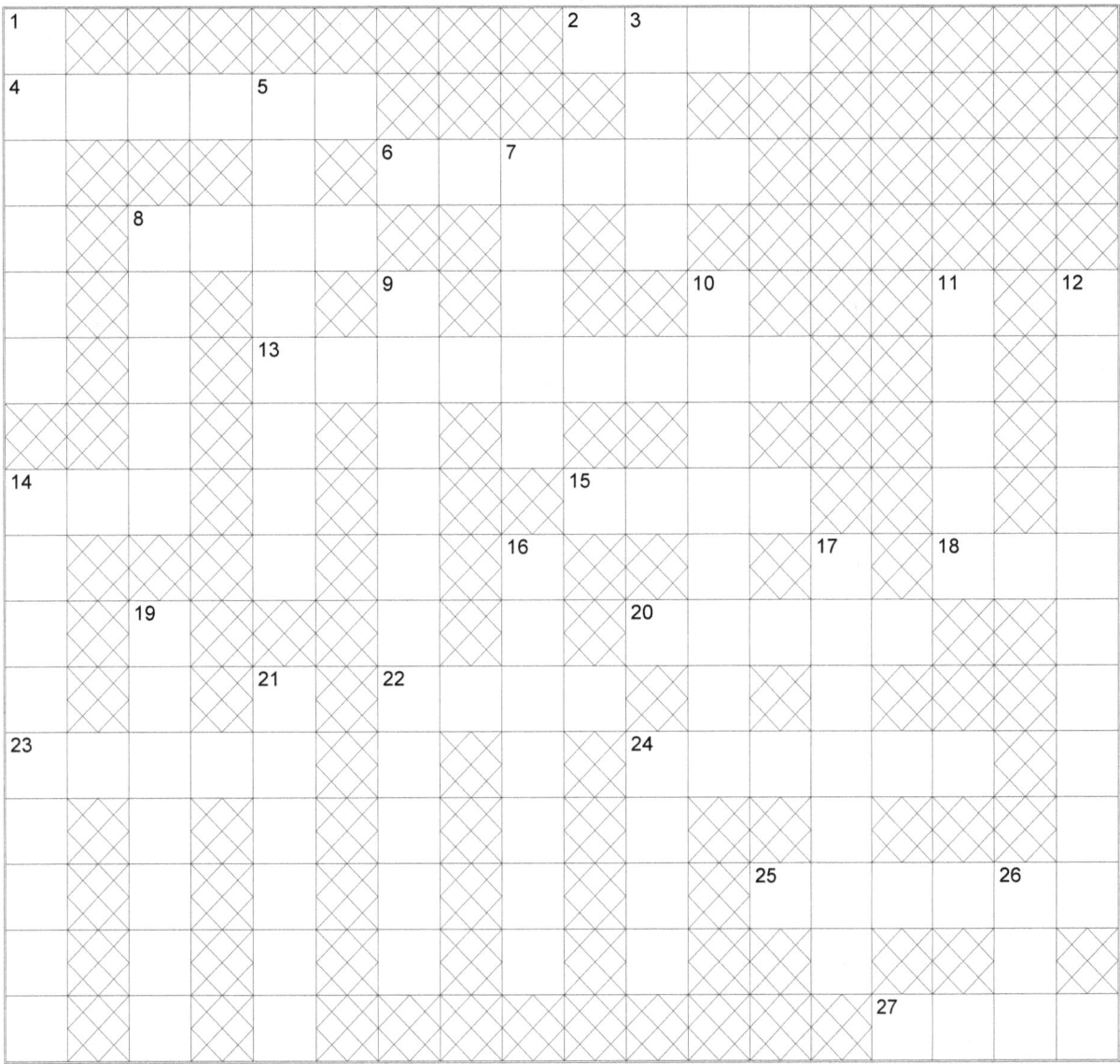

Across
2. Not bound
4. Montag's path to safety
6. He snatched books & hid them & got in trouble
8. Flames
13. Ear thimbles
14. Clarisse was hit & killed by one
15. Montag hid his books there after the ladies left.
18. Stop living
20. Remains after burning
22. Rain tasted like this beverage
23. Mildred took an overdose of sleeping ___.
24. Captain of the firemen
25. Fireman's head protector
27. Destroy with flames

Down
1. Montag was afraid the hounds would do this
3. What we do with books
5. It smelled like perfume to Montag
7. Time when most fires were set
8. He helped Montag
9. Mildred's pastime; huge television
10. She liked to think and talk
11. Mechanical ___; chased criminals
12. _____ 451
14. Harsh-sounding words
16. Flame starter
17. Transportation
19. Wife; informer; attempted suicide
21. To get away
24. One blew up the city
26. Place where radio transmitter was put for use

Fahrenheit 451 Crossword 2 Answer Key

	1 A								2 F	3 R	E	E		
4 T	R	A	5 K	S						E				
T			E			6 M	7 N	T	A	G				
A		8 F	I	R	E		I		D					
C		A		O	9 P		G		10 C		11 H		12 F
K		B	13 S	E	A	S	H	E	L	L	S		O		A
		E		E		R		T		A			U		H
14 C	A	R		N		L		15 Y	A	R	D		N		R
A				E		16 O		I			17 B		18 D	I	E
C		19 M				R		G		20 A	S	H	E	S		N
O		I		21 E	22 W	I	N	E		S		E				H
23 P	I	L	L	S		A	I		24 B	E	A	T	T	Y		E
H		D		C		L		T		O		L				I
O		R		A		L		E		25 M	H	E	L	26 M	E	T
N		E		P		S		R		B		S		A		
Y		D		E								27 B	U	R	N	

Across
2. Not bound
4. Montag's path to safety
6. He snatched books & hid them & got in trouble
8. Flames
13. Ear thimbles
14. Clarisse was hit & killed by one
15. Montag hid his books there after the ladies left.
18. Stop living
20. Remains after burning
22. Rain tasted like this beverage
23. Mildred took an overdose of sleeping ___.
24. Captain of the firemen
25. Fireman's head protector
27. Destroy with flames

7. Time when most fires were set
8. He helped Montag
9. Mildred's pastime; huge television
10. She liked to think and talk
11. Mechanical ___; chased criminals
12. _____ 451
14. Harsh-sounding words
16. Flame starter
17. Transportation
19. Wife; informer; attempted suicide
21. To get away
24. One blew up the city
26. Place where radio transmitter was put for use

Down
1. Montag was afraid the hounds would do this
3. What we do with books
5. It smelled like perfume to Montag

Fahrenheit 451 Crossword 3

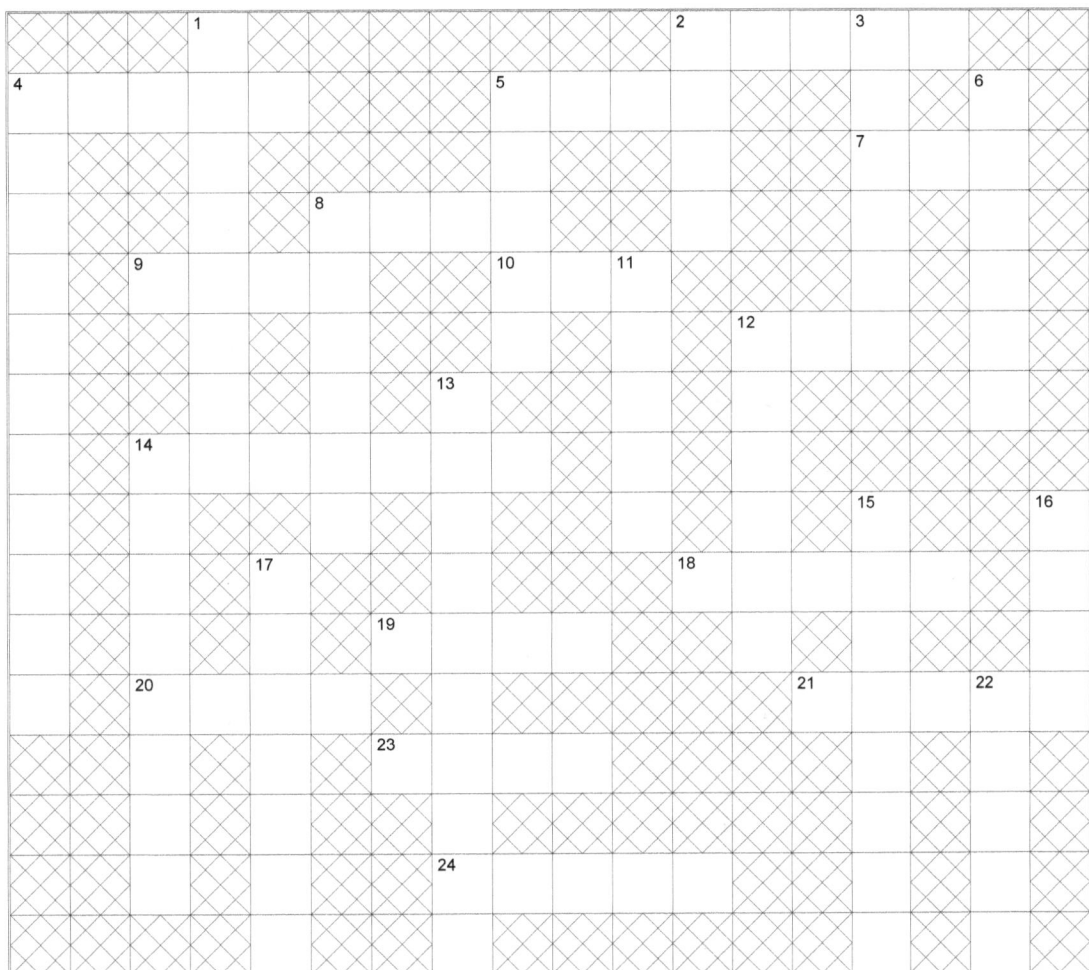

Across
2. Where Montag went after fleeing Faber's house
4. Mildred took an overdose of sleeping ___.
5. Not bound
7. Clarisse was hit & killed by one
8. One blew up the city
9. Rain tasted like this beverage
10. Place where radio transmitter was put for use
12. Stop living
14. Transportation
18. Remains after burning
19. Place where Montag met Faber
20. Destroy with flames
21. Mechanical ___; chased criminals
23. Flames
24. Montag took a book from the old lady's ___.

Down
1. She liked to think and talk
2. What we do with books
3. To get away
4. Mildred's pastime; huge television
5. He helped Montag
6. Montag's path to safety
8. Captain of the firemen
11. Small communications device used by Montag & Faber
12. Condensed version of a book
13. ____ Hound
14. Author
15. It smelled like perfume to Montag
16. Montag hid his books there after the ladies left.
17. They burned books & started fires
22. Time when most fires were set

Fahrenheit 451 Crossword 3 Answer Key

			1 C					2 R	I	V	3 E	R		
4 P	I	L	L	S		5 F	R	E	E		S		6 T	
A			A			A		A		7 C	A	R		
R			R		8 B	O	M	B		D		A		A
L		9 W	I	N	E		10 E	A	11 R		P		C	
O			S		A		R		A		12 D	I	E	K
R			S		T		13 M		D		I			S
W	14 B	E	E	T	L	E	S		I		G			
A	R			Y		C			O		E		15 K	16 Y
L	A		17 F		H			18 A	S	H	E	S		A
L	D		I		19 P	A	R	K		T		R		R
20 S	B	U	R	N		N				H	O	U	21 N	22 D
	U		E		23 F	I	R	E				S		I
	R		M		C							E		G
	Y		E		24 A	T	T	I	C			N		H
			N		L							E		T

Across
2. Where Montag went after fleeing Faber's house
4. Mildred took an overdose of sleeping ___.
5. Not bound
7. Clarisse was hit & killed by one
8. One blew up the city
9. Rain tasted like this beverage
10. Place where radio transmitter was put for use
12. Stop living
14. Transportation
18. Remains after burning
19. Place where Montag met Faber
20. Destroy with flames
21. Mechanical ___; chased criminals
23. Flames
24. Montag took a book from the old lady's ___.

Down
1. She liked to think and talk
2. What we do with books
3. To get away
4. Mildred's pastime; huge television
5. He helped Montag
6. Montag's path to safety
8. Captain of the firemen
11. Small communications device used by Montag & Faber
12. Condensed version of a book
13. ____ Hound
14. Author
15. It smelled like perfume to Montag
16. Montag hid his books there after the ladies left.
17. They burned books & started fires
22. Time when most fires were set

Fahrenheit 451 Crossword 4

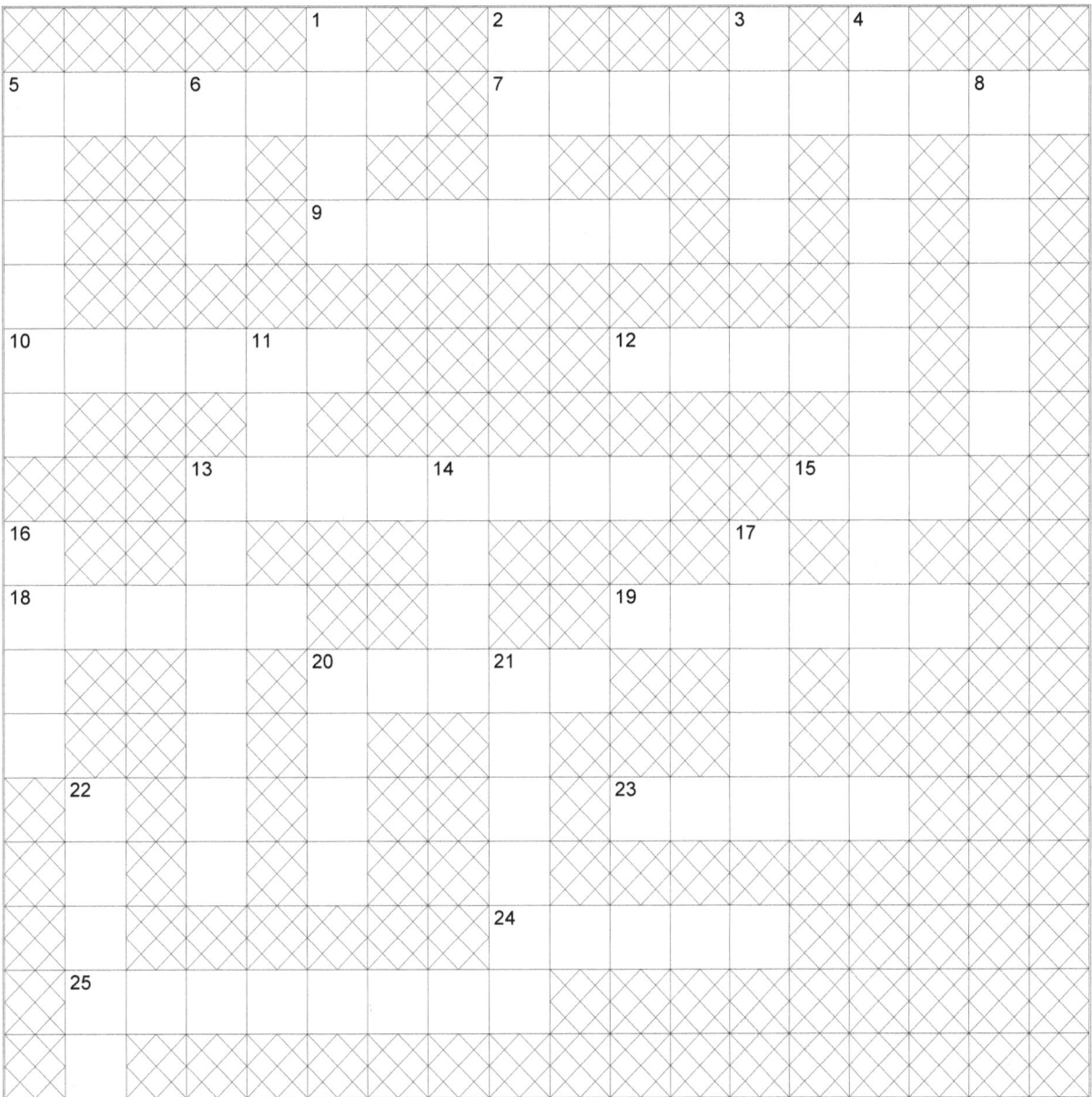

Across
 5. Wife; informer; attempted suicide
 7. People who told fireman who had books
 9. Condensed version of a book
10. Montag was afraid the hounds would do this
12. Where Montag went after fleeing Faber's house
13. Author
15. Place where radio transmitter was put for use
18. Remains after burning
19. Place Montag first hid his books
20. He helped Montag
23. Montag took a book from the old lady's ___.
24. Mildred took an overdose of sleeping ___.
25. It smelled like perfume to Montag

Down
 1. What we do with books
 2. Rain tasted like this beverage
 3. Not bound
 4. Mildred's pastime; huge television
 5. He snatched books & hid them & got in trouble
 6. Stop living
 8. Montag's path to safety
11. Clarisse was hit & killed by one
13. Transportation
14. One blew up the city
16. Montag hid his books there after the ladies left.
17. Time when most fires were set
20. Flames
21. To get away
22. Montag & Faber were going to plant these in firemen's houses

Fahrenheit 451 Crossword 4 Answer Key

				1 R		2 W			3 F		4 P	
5 M	I	L	6 D	R	E	D		7 I	N	F	O	R	M	A	N	8 T	S
O			I		A			N			E					R
N			E	9 D	I	G	E	S	T		E					A
T											O					C
10 A	T	T	11 A	C	K			12 R	I	V	E	R				K
G			A								W					S
			13 B	R	A	14 D	B	U	R	Y		15 E	A	R
16 Y			E			O					17 N		L
18 A	S	H	E	S		M		19 G	R	I	L	L	E
R				20 F	A	21 B	E	R			G		S
D				I				S			H	
	22 B	E	R		23 A	T	T	I	C
	O		S		E			A
	O			24 P	I	L	L	S
25 K	E	R	O	S	E	N	E
	S

Across

5. Wife; informer; attempted suicide
7. People who told fireman who had books
9. Condensed version of a book
10. Montag was afraid the hounds would do this
12. Where Montag went after fleeing Faber's house
13. Author
15. Place where radio transmitter was put for use
18. Remains after burning
19. Place Montag first hid his books
20. He helped Montag
23. Montag took a book from the old lady's ___.
24. Mildred took an overdose of sleeping ___.
25. It smelled like perfume to Montag

Down

1. What we do with books
2. Rain tasted like this beverage
3. Not bound
4. Mildred's pastime; huge television
5. He snatched books & hid them & got in trouble
6. Stop living
8. Montag's path to safety
11. Clarisse was hit & killed by one
13. Transportation
14. One blew up the city
16. Montag hid his books there after the ladies left.
17. Time when most fires were set
20. Flames
21. To get away
22. Montag & Faber were going to plant these in firemen's houses

Fahrenheit 451

INFORMANTS	PHOENIX	FREE	DIGEST	BEATTY
FIREMEN	LOUIS	ATTACK	KEROSENE	CACOPHONY
HOUND	WINE	FREE SPACE	SEASHELLS	BURN
YARD	ESCAPE	RIVER	FIRE	NIGHT
MECHANICAL	PILLS	ASHES	EAR	INCINERATOR

Fahrenheit 451

CAR	HOBOS	CLARISSE	RADIO	MILDRED
BOOKS	HELMET	TRACKS	DIE	IGNITER
PARLORWALLS	BRADBURY	FREE SPACE	ATTIC	BEETLES
GRILLE	MONTAG	READ	BOMB	FAHRENHEIT
PARK	INCINERATOR	EAR	ASHES	PILLS

Fahrenheit 451

INCINERATOR	CAR	LOUIS	FIREMEN	BEATTY
PHOENIX	BOOKS	CLARISSE	ATTACK	ECCLESIASTES
BEETLES	FABER	FREE SPACE	NIGHT	ASHES
HOUND	SEASHELLS	MECHANICAL	MONTAG	KEROSENE
BOMB	RADIO	EAR	BURN	PARLORWALLS

Fahrenheit 451

YARD	TRACKS	WINE	MILDRED	FIRE
RIVER	HOBOS	PARK	CACOPHONY	PILLS
ATTIC	FREE	FREE SPACE	INFORMANTS	BRADBURY
ESCAPE	HELMET	READ	DIE	IGNITER
GRILLE	PARLORWALLS	BURN	EAR	RADIO

Fahrenheit 451

KEROSENE	GRILLE	IGNITER	LOUIS	RADIO
NIGHT	HELMET	BRADBURY	PARLORWALLS	HOUND
MECHANICAL	DIGEST	FREE SPACE	FREE	FIREMEN
CLARISSE	ATTIC	ATTACK	ECCLESIASTES	BURN
PHOENIX	WINE	PARK	CACOPHONY	PILLS

Fahrenheit 451

ASHES	TRACKS	FABER	BEETLES	EAR
HOBOS	FAHRENHEIT	BOOKS	INCINERATOR	ESCAPE
READ	BEATTY	FREE SPACE	YARD	DIE
SEASHELLS	CAR	RIVER	FIRE	MILDRED
MONTAG	PILLS	CACOPHONY	PARK	WINE

Fahrenheit 451

BOOKS	MILDRED	FREE	NIGHT	KEROSENE
PILLS	BEATTY	CACOPHONY	PHOENIX	FIRE
PARLORWALLS	HELMET	FREE SPACE	DIE	CLARISSE
BOMB	MONTAG	MECHANICAL	RADIO	FAHRENHEIT
CAR	WINE	GRILLE	HOUND	ATTACK

Fahrenheit 451

DIGEST	INCINERATOR	ASHES	ESCAPE	PARK
FIREMEN	ECCLESIASTES	READ	INFORMANTS	EAR
YARD	RIVER	FREE SPACE	FABER	IGNITER
ATTIC	BEETLES	BRADBURY	SEASHELLS	BURN
TRACKS	ATTACK	HOUND	GRILLE	WINE

Fahrenheit 451

CACOPHONY	PARK	DIE	EAR	ECCLESIASTES
PHOENIX	FIREMEN	LOUIS	BOMB	INCINERATOR
ATTIC	MILDRED	FREE SPACE	FAHRENHEIT	PARLORWALLS
WINE	FREE	BOOKS	READ	GRILLE
BEETLES	NIGHT	TRACKS	FABER	ASHES

Fahrenheit 451

INFORMANTS	FIRE	DIGEST	MECHANICAL	PILLS
IGNITER	HOBOS	CLARISSE	ESCAPE	CAR
BURN	KEROSENE	FREE SPACE	YARD	BRADBURY
HOUND	ATTACK	HELMET	SEASHELLS	RADIO
BEATTY	ASHES	FABER	TRACKS	NIGHT

Fahrenheit 451

RIVER	KEROSENE	PARLORWALLS	IGNITER	BOMB
MONTAG	INFORMANTS	EAR	MECHANICAL	PHOENIX
PARK	READ	FREE SPACE	BEATTY	BRADBURY
HOUND	ATTIC	DIGEST	WINE	NIGHT
ESCAPE	PILLS	FIRE	BURN	INCINERATOR

Fahrenheit 451

HELMET	CACOPHONY	DIE	FIREMEN	FABER
LOUIS	TRACKS	FAHRENHEIT	GRILLE	FREE
ATTACK	BOOKS	FREE SPACE	CLARISSE	MILDRED
ASHES	RADIO	CAR	BEETLES	YARD
ECCLESIASTES	INCINERATOR	BURN	FIRE	PILLS

Fahrenheit 451

BOOKS	IGNITER	CLARISSE	DIE	DIGEST
KEROSENE	MILDRED	SEASHELLS	BOMB	BEATTY
HOUND	NIGHT	FREE SPACE	CAR	ATTACK
ECCLESIASTES	ATTIC	CACOPHONY	PILLS	FAHRENHEIT
TRACKS	READ	RADIO	YARD	FIRE

Fahrenheit 451

HELMET	RIVER	INCINERATOR	MONTAG	ASHES
HOBOS	GRILLE	BURN	EAR	BEETLES
PHOENIX	FIREMEN	FREE SPACE	FREE	BRADBURY
MECHANICAL	FABER	INFORMANTS	ESCAPE	PARK
PARLORWALLS	FIRE	YARD	RADIO	READ

Fahrenheit 451

PILLS	DIE	FIREMEN	DIGEST	HOBOS
MECHANICAL	RADIO	SEASHELLS	INCINERATOR	WINE
PHOENIX	HOUND	FREE SPACE	FIRE	HELMET
KEROSENE	TRACKS	PARK	FAHRENHEIT	MONTAG
ASHES	BOOKS	CLARISSE	ATTACK	ATTIC

Fahrenheit 451

GRILLE	INFORMANTS	FREE	IGNITER	BEETLES
LOUIS	CACOPHONY	RIVER	EAR	ESCAPE
NIGHT	BEATTY	FREE SPACE	READ	PARLORWALLS
MILDRED	YARD	CAR	BOMB	BURN
ECCLESIASTES	ATTIC	ATTACK	CLARISSE	BOOKS

Fahrenheit 451

TRACKS	HOUND	CAR	SEASHELLS	HELMET
CACOPHONY	YARD	LOUIS	BOMB	FREE
FIREMEN	PARK	FREE SPACE	BOOKS	PILLS
MILDRED	PHOENIX	BEATTY	EAR	DIE
ECCLESIASTES	GRILLE	MECHANICAL	WINE	NIGHT

Fahrenheit 451

MONTAG	DIGEST	FABER	BEETLES	RADIO
PARLORWALLS	ATTIC	HOBOS	IGNITER	INCINERATOR
FAHRENHEIT	BURN	FREE SPACE	ASHES	FIRE
ATTACK	KEROSENE	RIVER	ESCAPE	BRADBURY
READ	NIGHT	WINE	MECHANICAL	GRILLE

Fahrenheit 451

SEASHELLS	FIREMEN	NIGHT	RADIO	HELMET
BOOKS	BEATTY	ATTIC	HOUND	CLARISSE
FREE	ECCLESIASTES	FREE SPACE	HOBOS	KEROSENE
MECHANICAL	BRADBURY	TRACKS	ESCAPE	FIRE
FAHRENHEIT	READ	DIE	CACOPHONY	MONTAG

Fahrenheit 451

BEETLES	MILDRED	YARD	EAR	ASHES
INCINERATOR	BURN	GRILLE	BOMB	DIGEST
FABER	PARK	FREE SPACE	PILLS	LOUIS
RIVER	WINE	PHOENIX	ATTACK	PARLORWALLS
CAR	MONTAG	CACOPHONY	DIE	READ

Fahrenheit 451

CAR	TRACKS	BOOKS	PARLORWALLS	ATTACK
ASHES	BEETLES	DIE	BRADBURY	DIGEST
RIVER	ATTIC	FREE SPACE	PHOENIX	FABER
BURN	FAHRENHEIT	NIGHT	CACOPHONY	WINE
EAR	ESCAPE	READ	ECCLESIASTES	MECHANICAL

Fahrenheit 451

FREE	KEROSENE	PARK	FIREMEN	LOUIS
INFORMANTS	PILLS	MILDRED	CLARISSE	BOMB
HOBOS	MONTAG	FREE SPACE	HOUND	RADIO
IGNITER	YARD	INCINERATOR	HELMET	BEATTY
GRILLE	MECHANICAL	ECCLESIASTES	READ	ESCAPE

Fahrenheit 451

FAHRENHEIT	RIVER	MECHANICAL	BEATTY	CACOPHONY
RADIO	GRILLE	EAR	BOMB	ATTACK
BURN	DIE	FREE SPACE	ATTIC	PILLS
CAR	CLARISSE	SEASHELLS	YARD	INCINERATOR
HOUND	PARK	KEROSENE	ASHES	ECCLESIASTES

Fahrenheit 451

FABER	PARLORWALLS	FIRE	TRACKS	FREE
PHOENIX	BOOKS	READ	MONTAG	FIREMEN
BEETLES	ESCAPE	FREE SPACE	INFORMANTS	LOUIS
HOBOS	BRADBURY	DIGEST	MILDRED	WINE
NIGHT	ECCLESIASTES	ASHES	KEROSENE	PARK

Fahrenheit 451

BOOKS	PHOENIX	KEROSENE	PARK	TRACKS
BEATTY	ASHES	PARLORWALLS	FREE	FIRE
NIGHT	YARD	FREE SPACE	HELMET	ATTACK
FABER	CLARISSE	ESCAPE	BEETLES	IGNITER
CACOPHONY	MILDRED	INCINERATOR	CAR	DIGEST

Fahrenheit 451

RIVER	BOMB	HOUND	BURN	ECCLESIASTES
DIE	LOUIS	WINE	INFORMANTS	HOBOS
BRADBURY	RADIO	FREE SPACE	FAHRENHEIT	SEASHELLS
EAR	READ	FIREMEN	PILLS	GRILLE
MECHANICAL	DIGEST	CAR	INCINERATOR	MILDRED

Fahrenheit 451

INCINERATOR	MECHANICAL	YARD	BEATTY	GRILLE
INFORMANTS	MONTAG	DIGEST	RIVER	FABER
FREE	FIRE	FREE SPACE	ATTIC	PARK
RADIO	WINE	CAR	EAR	BURN
ATTACK	ASHES	HOUND	BEETLES	ESCAPE

Fahrenheit 451

IGNITER	BOOKS	KEROSENE	FIREMEN	BOMB
PHOENIX	READ	CACOPHONY	FAHRENHEIT	BRADBURY
TRACKS	CLARISSE	FREE SPACE	PARLORWALLS	DIE
MILDRED	ECCLESIASTES	HOBOS	HELMET	LOUIS
SEASHELLS	ESCAPE	BEETLES	HOUND	ASHES

Fahrenheit 451

INCINERATOR	TRACKS	HOUND	IGNITER	DIE
DIGEST	FREE	READ	WINE	RIVER
FIRE	EAR	FREE SPACE	MECHANICAL	PARK
HOBOS	BOOKS	KEROSENE	ASHES	FAHRENHEIT
LOUIS	CACOPHONY	SEASHELLS	CAR	FIREMEN

Fahrenheit 451

YARD	ESCAPE	BURN	ATTACK	HELMET
PARLORWALLS	ATTIC	CLARISSE	BEETLES	RADIO
BOMB	ECCLESIASTES	FREE SPACE	GRILLE	PHOENIX
MONTAG	NIGHT	FABER	BRADBURY	PILLS
BEATTY	FIREMEN	CAR	SEASHELLS	CACOPHONY

Fahrenheit 451

LOUIS	INCINERATOR	FABER	HOBOS	ATTIC
MILDRED	HELMET	DIE	RIVER	FIREMEN
TRACKS	MECHANICAL	FREE SPACE	YARD	WINE
GRILLE	ESCAPE	PILLS	READ	FREE
BOOKS	KEROSENE	DIGEST	NIGHT	ECCLESIASTES

Fahrenheit 451

ATTACK	CACOPHONY	PARK	BOMB	IGNITER
SEASHELLS	BURN	MONTAG	FIRE	EAR
CAR	RADIO	FREE SPACE	INFORMANTS	BEATTY
PHOENIX	HOUND	PARLORWALLS	FAHRENHEIT	BEETLES
BRADBURY	ECCLESIASTES	NIGHT	DIGEST	KEROSENE

Fahrenheit 451 Vocabulary Word List

No.	Word	Clue/Definition
1.	BALLISTICS	The study of the dynamics of projectiles
2.	CADENCED	With a rhythmic flow
3.	CAPILLARY	Fine; small in diameter
4.	CARDAMON	Indian Spice
5.	CENTRIFUGE	Apparatus consisting of a compartment spun around a central axis
6.	COWARDICE	Lacks courage in the face of danger
7.	DICTUM	Authoritative pronouncement
8.	ERECTED	Set up; established
9.	GROTESQUE	Bizarre; distorted
10.	IMPERCEPTIBLY	Impossible to detect by ordinary senses
11.	INDECISIVE	Not able to make a decision
12.	JUGGERNAUT	Overwhelming, advancing sight crushing all in its path
13.	LIMNED	Described
14.	MANIFESTED	Showed; revealed
15.	MELANCHOLY	Sadness; gloominess
16.	MULTIFACETED	Having many faces
17.	NONCOMBUSTIBLE	Does not burn easily
18.	OBSCURE	Not readily noticed or seen; not commonly known
19.	ODIOUS	Arousing strong dislike or displeasure
20.	PARRIED	Deflected; avoided
21.	PEDANTS	Those who flaunt their knowledge
22.	PRATFALL	Humiliating failure; a fall on the buttocks
23.	PROCLIVITIES	Predispositions; tendencies
24.	PULVERIZED	Reduced to powder
25.	PYRE	A pile of combustible materials for burning a corpse
26.	RAVENOUS	Extremely hungry; greedy for gratification
27.	RECEPTACLE	A container that holds matter
28.	REFRACTED	Deflected from a straight path
29.	RETALIATION	Returning like for like, especially evil
30.	SIMULTANEOUSLY	Happening at the same time
31.	SMOLDERING	Burning with little smoke and no flame
32.	STOLID	Having or revealing little emotion
33.	TACTILE	Relating to the sense of touch
34.	VERBIAGE	Wordiness

Fahrenheit 451 Vocabulary Fill In The Blank 1

_____ 1. Overwhelming, advancing sight crushing all in its path

_____ 2. Not able to make a decision

_____ 3. Deflected; avoided

_____ 4. Impossible to detect by ordinary senses

_____ 5. Deflected from a straight path

_____ 6. Arousing strong dislike or displeasure

_____ 7. Those who flaunt their knowledge

_____ 8. Happening at the same time

_____ 9. Indian Spice

_____ 10. A container that holds matter

_____ 11. Apparatus consisting of a compartment spun around a central axis

_____ 12. Bizarre; distorted

_____ 13. Predispositions; tendencies

_____ 14. Fine; small in diameter

_____ 15. Extremely hungry; greedy for gratification

_____ 16. Sadness; gloominess

_____ 17. Having or revealing little emotion

_____ 18. Authoritative pronouncement

_____ 19. Burning with little smoke and no flame

_____ 20. Having many faces

Fahrenheit 451 Vocabulary Fill In The Blank 1 Answer Key

JUGGERNAUT	1. Overwhelming, advancing sight crushing all in its path
INDECISIVE	2. Not able to make a decision
PARRIED	3. Deflected; avoided
IMPERCEPTIBLY	4. Impossible to detect by ordinary senses
REFRACTED	5. Deflected from a straight path
ODIOUS	6. Arousing strong dislike or displeasure
PEDANTS	7. Those who flaunt their knowledge
SIMULTANEOUSLY	8. Happening at the same time
CARDAMON	9. Indian Spice
RECEPTACLE	10. A container that holds matter
CENTRIFUGE	11. Apparatus consisting of a compartment spun around a central axis
GROTESQUE	12. Bizarre; distorted
PROCLIVITIES	13. Predispositions; tendencies
CAPILLARY	14. Fine; small in diameter
RAVENOUS	15. Extremely hungry; greedy for gratification
MELANCHOLY	16. Sadness; gloominess
STOLID	17. Having or revealing little emotion
DICTUM	18. Authoritative pronouncement
SMOLDERING	19. Burning with little smoke and no flame
MULTIFACETED	20. Having many faces

Fahrenheit 451 Vocabulary Fill In The Blank 2

_____ 1. Overwhelming, advancing sight crushing all in its path

_____ 2. Burning with little smoke and no flame

_____ 3. Apparatus consisting of a compartment spun around a central axis

_____ 4. Deflected; avoided

_____ 5. Not readily noticed or seen; not commonly known

_____ 6. Returning like for like, especially evil

_____ 7. Not able to make a decision

_____ 8. Deflected from a straight path

_____ 9. Fine; small in diameter

_____ 10. Relating to the sense of touch

_____ 11. Does not burn easily

_____ 12. Indian Spice

_____ 13. With a rhythmic flow

_____ 14. Bizarre; distorted

_____ 15. Described

_____ 16. Authoritative pronouncement

_____ 17. A pile of combustible materials for burning a corpse

_____ 18. Reduced to powder

_____ 19. Humiliating failure; a fall on the buttocks

_____ 20. Set up; established

Fahrenheit 451 Vocabulary Fill In The Blank 2 Answer Key

JUGGERNAUT	1. Overwhelming, advancing sight crushing all in its path
SMOLDERING	2. Burning with little smoke and no flame
CENTRIFUGE	3. Apparatus consisting of a compartment spun around a central axis
PARRIED	4. Deflected; avoided
OBSCURE	5. Not readily noticed or seen; not commonly known
RETALIATION	6. Returning like for like, especially evil
INDECISIVE	7. Not able to make a decision
REFRACTED	8. Deflected from a straight path
CAPILLARY	9. Fine; small in diameter
TACTILE	10. Relating to the sense of touch
NONCOMBUSTIBLE	11. Does not burn easily
CARDAMON	12. Indian Spice
CADENCED	13. With a rhythmic flow
GROTESQUE	14. Bizarre; distorted
LIMNED	15. Described
DICTUM	16. Authoritative pronouncement
PYRE	17. A pile of combustible materials for burning a corpse
PULVERIZED	18. Reduced to powder
PRATFALL	19. Humiliating failure; a fall on the buttocks
ERECTED	20. Set up; established

Fahrenheit 451 Vocabulary Fill In The Blank 3

_____ 1. Apparatus consisting of a compartment spun around a central axis
_____ 2. Burning with little smoke and no flame
_____ 3. Showed; revealed
_____ 4. Deflected from a straight path
_____ 5. Those who flaunt their knowledge
_____ 6. Returning like for like, especially evil
_____ 7. Bizarre; distorted
_____ 8. Happening at the same time
_____ 9. A pile of combustible materials for burning a corpse
_____ 10. Extremely hungry; greedy for gratification
_____ 11. Not readily noticed or seen; not commonly known
_____ 12. Indian Spice
_____ 13. Deflected; avoided
_____ 14. Fine; small in diameter
_____ 15. Having or revealing little emotion
_____ 16. The study of the dynamics of projectiles
_____ 17. Predispositions; tendencies
_____ 18. Not able to make a decision
_____ 19. Relating to the sense of touch
_____ 20. Set up; established

Fahrenheit 451 Vocabulary Fill In The Blank 3 Answer Key

CENTRIFUGE	1. Apparatus consisting of a compartment spun around a central axis
SMOLDERING	2. Burning with little smoke and no flame
MANIFESTED	3. Showed; revealed
REFRACTED	4. Deflected from a straight path
PEDANTS	5. Those who flaunt their knowledge
RETALIATION	6. Returning like for like, especially evil
GROTESQUE	7. Bizarre; distorted
SIMULTANEOUSLY	8. Happening at the same time
PYRE	9. A pile of combustible materials for burning a corpse
RAVENOUS	10. Extremely hungry; greedy for gratification
OBSCURE	11. Not readily noticed or seen; not commonly known
CARDAMON	12. Indian Spice
PARRIED	13. Deflected; avoided
CAPILLARY	14. Fine; small in diameter
STOLID	15. Having or revealing little emotion
BALLISTICS	16. The study of the dynamics of projectiles
PROCLIVITIES	17. Predispositions; tendencies
INDECISIVE	18. Not able to make a decision
TACTILE	19. Relating to the sense of touch
ERECTED	20. Set up; established

Fahrenheit 451 Vocabulary Fill In The Blank 4

_____ 1. The study of the dynamics of projectiles

_____ 2. Authoritative pronouncement

_____ 3. Showed; revealed

_____ 4. A container that holds matter

_____ 5. Indian Spice

_____ 6. Deflected; avoided

_____ 7. Predispositions; tendencies

_____ 8. A pile of combustible materials for burning a corpse

_____ 9. Bizarre; distorted

_____ 10. Deflected from a straight path

_____ 11. Relating to the sense of touch

_____ 12. Does not burn easily

_____ 13. With a rhythmic flow

_____ 14. Arousing strong dislike or displeasure

_____ 15. Returning like for like, especially evil

_____ 16. Having many faces

_____ 17. Impossible to detect by ordinary senses

_____ 18. Sadness; gloominess

_____ 19. Those who flaunt their knowledge

_____ 20. Reduced to powder

Fahrenheit 451 Vocabulary Fill In The Blank 4 Answer Key

BALLISTICS	1. The study of the dynamics of projectiles
DICTUM	2. Authoritative pronouncement
MANIFESTED	3. Showed; revealed
RECEPTACLE	4. A container that holds matter
CARDAMON	5. Indian Spice
PARRIED	6. Deflected; avoided
PROCLIVITIES	7. Predispositions; tendencies
PYRE	8. A pile of combustible materials for burning a corpse
GROTESQUE	9. Bizarre; distorted
REFRACTED	10. Deflected from a straight path
TACTILE	11. Relating to the sense of touch
NONCOMBUSTIBLE	12. Does not burn easily
CADENCED	13. With a rhythmic flow
ODIOUS	14. Arousing strong dislike or displeasure
RETALIATION	15. Returning like for like, especially evil
MULTIFACETED	16. Having many faces
IMPERCEPTIBLY	17. Impossible to detect by ordinary senses
MELANCHOLY	18. Sadness; gloominess
PEDANTS	19. Those who flaunt their knowledge
PULVERIZED	20. Reduced to powder

Fahrenheit 451 Vocabulary Matching 1

___ 1. DICTUM   A. A pile of combustible materials for burning a corpse
___ 2. GROTESQUE   B. Those who flaunt their knowledge
___ 3. CADENCED   C. Deflected; avoided
___ 4. COWARDICE   D. Having many faces
___ 5. MULTIFACETED   E. Showed; revealed
___ 6. PULVERIZED   F. Lacks courage in the face of danger
___ 7. PEDANTS   G. Returning like for like, especially evil
___ 8. PROCLIVITIES   H. Not able to make a decision
___ 9. CAPILLARY   I. The study of the dynamics of projectiles
___10. LIMNED   J. Wordiness
___11. INDECISIVE   K. Deflected from a straight path
___12. IMPERCEPTIBLY   L. Bizarre; distorted
___13. PARRIED   M. Set up; established
___14. CARDAMON   N. With a rhythmic flow
___15. REFRACTED   O. Impossible to detect by ordinary senses
___16. PYRE   P. Fine; small in diameter
___17. ERECTED   Q. Predispositions; tendencies
___18. TACTILE   R. Reduced to powder
___19. OBSCURE   S. Burning with little smoke and no flame
___20. SMOLDERING   T. Indian Spice
___21. RETALIATION   U. Having or revealing little emotion
___22. VERBIAGE   V. Authoritative pronouncement
___23. MANIFESTED   W. Not readily noticed or seen; not commonly known
___24. STOLID   X. Relating to the sense of touch
___25. BALLISTICS   Y. Described

Fahrenheit 451 Vocabulary Matching 1 Answer Key

V - 1.	DICTUM	A. A pile of combustible materials for burning a corpse
L - 2.	GROTESQUE	B. Those who flaunt their knowledge
N - 3.	CADENCED	C. Deflected; avoided
F - 4.	COWARDICE	D. Having many faces
D - 5.	MULTIFACETED	E. Showed; revealed
R - 6.	PULVERIZED	F. Lacks courage in the face of danger
B - 7.	PEDANTS	G. Returning like for like, especially evil
Q - 8.	PROCLIVITIES	H. Not able to make a decision
P - 9.	CAPILLARY	I. The study of the dynamics of projectiles
Y - 10.	LIMNED	J. Wordiness
H - 11.	INDECISIVE	K. Deflected from a straight path
O - 12.	IMPERCEPTIBLY	L. Bizarre; distorted
C - 13.	PARRIED	M. Set up; established
T - 14.	CARDAMON	N. With a rhythmic flow
K - 15.	REFRACTED	O. Impossible to detect by ordinary senses
A - 16.	PYRE	P. Fine; small in diameter
M - 17.	ERECTED	Q. Predispositions; tendencies
X - 18.	TACTILE	R. Reduced to powder
W - 19.	OBSCURE	S. Burning with little smoke and no flame
S - 20.	SMOLDERING	T. Indian Spice
G - 21.	RETALIATION	U. Having or revealing little emotion
J - 22.	VERBIAGE	V. Authoritative pronouncement
E - 23.	MANIFESTED	W. Not readily noticed or seen; not commonly known
U - 24.	STOLID	X. Relating to the sense of touch
I - 25.	BALLISTICS	Y. Described

Fahrenheit 451 Vocabulary Matching 2

___ 1. CENTRIFUGE   A. Showed; revealed
___ 2. STOLID   B. Impossible to detect by ordinary senses
___ 3. CADENCED   C. A pile of combustible materials for burning a corpse
___ 4. RECEPTACLE   D. Happening at the same time
___ 5. CAPILLARY   E. Lacks courage in the face of danger
___ 6. GROTESQUE   F. Wordiness
___ 7. PYRE   G. Reduced to powder
___ 8. PROCLIVITIES   H. Indian Spice
___ 9. IMPERCEPTIBLY   I. With a rhythmic flow
___10. VERBIAGE   J. Authoritative pronouncement
___11. MULTIFACETED   K. Having or revealing little emotion
___12. ERECTED   L. Sadness; gloominess
___13. BALLISTICS   M. Deflected; avoided
___14. SIMULTANEOUSLY   N. Set up; established
___15. COWARDICE   O. A container that holds matter
___16. MANIFESTED   P. Predispositions; tendencies
___17. RETALIATION   Q. Apparatus consisting of a compartment spun around a central axis
___18. MELANCHOLY   R. The study of the dynamics of projectiles
___19. ODIOUS   S. Fine; small in diameter
___20. PULVERIZED   T. Relating to the sense of touch
___21. TACTILE   U. Bizarre; distorted
___22. CARDAMON   V. Having many faces
___23. DICTUM   W. Arousing strong dislike or displeasure
___24. PARRIED   X. Not readily noticed or seen; not commonly known
___25. OBSCURE   Y. Returning like for like, especially evil

Fahrenheit 451 Vocabulary Matching 2 Answer Key

Q - 1.	CENTRIFUGE	A. Showed; revealed
K - 2.	STOLID	B. Impossible to detect by ordinary senses
I - 3.	CADENCED	C. A pile of combustible materials for burning a corpse
O - 4.	RECEPTACLE	D. Happening at the same time
S - 5.	CAPILLARY	E. Lacks courage in the face of danger
U - 6.	GROTESQUE	F. Wordiness
C - 7.	PYRE	G. Reduced to powder
P - 8.	PROCLIVITIES	H. Indian Spice
B - 9.	IMPERCEPTIBLY	I. With a rhythmic flow
F - 10.	VERBIAGE	J. Authoritative pronouncement
V - 11.	MULTIFACETED	K. Having or revealing little emotion
N - 12.	ERECTED	L. Sadness; gloominess
R - 13.	BALLISTICS	M. Deflected; avoided
D - 14.	SIMULTANEOUSLY	N. Set up; established
E - 15.	COWARDICE	O. A container that holds matter
A - 16.	MANIFESTED	P. Predispositions; tendencies
Y - 17.	RETALIATION	Q. Apparatus consisting of a compartment spun around a central axis
L - 18.	MELANCHOLY	R. The study of the dynamics of projectiles
W - 19.	ODIOUS	S. Fine; small in diameter
G - 20.	PULVERIZED	T. Relating to the sense of touch
T - 21.	TACTILE	U. Bizarre; distorted
H - 22.	CARDAMON	V. Having many faces
J - 23.	DICTUM	W. Arousing strong dislike or displeasure
M - 24.	PARRIED	X. Not readily noticed or seen; not commonly known
X - 25.	OBSCURE	Y. Returning like for like, especially evil

Fahrenheit 451 Vocabulary Matching 3

___ 1. SIMULTANEOUSLY   A. Having or revealing little emotion
___ 2. PROCLIVITIES   B. Arousing strong dislike or displeasure
___ 3. MULTIFACETED   C. Authoritative pronouncement
___ 4. RECEPTACLE   D. Not readily noticed or seen; not commonly known
___ 5. STOLID   E. Described
___ 6. PRATFALL   F. Bizarre; distorted
___ 7. DICTUM   G. Lacks courage in the face of danger
___ 8. PULVERIZED   H. Apparatus consisting of a compartment spun around a central axis
___ 9. CENTRIFUGE   I. Those who flaunt their knowledge
___10. ERECTED   J. Relating to the sense of touch
___11. OBSCURE   K. Deflected from a straight path
___12. JUGGERNAUT   L. Overwhelming, advancing sight crushing all in its path
___13. CAPILLARY   M. A container that holds matter
___14. ODIOUS   N. Humiliating failure; a fall on the buttocks
___15. INDECISIVE   O. Impossible to detect by ordinary senses
___16. IMPERCEPTIBLY   P. Indian Spice
___17. VERBIAGE   Q. Predispositions; tendencies
___18. BALLISTICS   R. Set up; established
___19. CARDAMON   S. Reduced to powder
___20. COWARDICE   T. Happening at the same time
___21. LIMNED   U. The study of the dynamics of projectiles
___22. REFRACTED   V. Having many faces
___23. GROTESQUE   W. Fine; small in diameter
___24. PEDANTS   X. Not able to make a decision
___25. TACTILE   Y. Wordiness

Fahrenheit 451 Vocabulary Matching 3 Answer Key

T - 1. SIMULTANEOUSLY	A.	Having or revealing little emotion
Q - 2. PROCLIVITIES	B.	Arousing strong dislike or displeasure
V - 3. MULTIFACETED	C.	Authoritative pronouncement
M - 4. RECEPTACLE	D.	Not readily noticed or seen; not commonly known
A - 5. STOLID	E.	Described
N - 6. PRATFALL	F.	Bizarre; distorted
C - 7. DICTUM	G.	Lacks courage in the face of danger
S - 8. PULVERIZED	H.	Apparatus consisting of a compartment spun around a central axis
H - 9. CENTRIFUGE	I.	Those who flaunt their knowledge
R -10. ERECTED	J.	Relating to the sense of touch
D -11. OBSCURE	K.	Deflected from a straight path
L -12. JUGGERNAUT	L.	Overwhelming, advancing sight crushing all in its path
W -13. CAPILLARY	M.	A container that holds matter
B -14. ODIOUS	N.	Humiliating failure; a fall on the buttocks
X -15. INDECISIVE	O.	Impossible to detect by ordinary senses
O -16. IMPERCEPTIBLY	P.	Indian Spice
Y -17. VERBIAGE	Q.	Predispositions; tendencies
U -18. BALLISTICS	R.	Set up; established
P -19. CARDAMON	S.	Reduced to powder
G -20. COWARDICE	T.	Happening at the same time
E -21. LIMNED	U.	The study of the dynamics of projectiles
K -22. REFRACTED	V.	Having many faces
F -23. GROTESQUE	W.	Fine; small in diameter
I - 24. PEDANTS	X.	Not able to make a decision
J - 25. TACTILE	Y.	Wordiness

Fahrenheit 451 Vocabulary Matching 4

___ 1. PYRE   A. Reduced to powder
___ 2. PROCLIVITIES   B. Showed; revealed
___ 3. ODIOUS   C. Not able to make a decision
___ 4. DICTUM   D. Wordiness
___ 5. CARDAMON   E. Predispositions; tendencies
___ 6. SMOLDERING   F. Not readily noticed or seen; not commonly known
___ 7. LIMNED   G. Burning with little smoke and no flame
___ 8. PULVERIZED   H. Deflected; avoided
___ 9. STOLID   I. The study of the dynamics of projectiles
___10. MULTIFACETED   J. Overwhelming, advancing sight crushing all in its path
___11. INDECISIVE   K. Relating to the sense of touch
___12. PEDANTS   L. Indian Spice
___13. RAVENOUS   M. With a rhythmic flow
___14. PRATFALL   N. Having or revealing little emotion
___15. OBSCURE   O. Having many faces
___16. MANIFESTED   P. Extremely hungry; greedy for gratification
___17. VERBIAGE   Q. A pile of combustible materials for burning a corpse
___18. RETALIATION   R. Set up; established
___19. BALLISTICS   S. Those who flaunt their knowledge
___20. JUGGERNAUT   T. Arousing strong dislike or displeasure
___21. PARRIED   U. Authoritative pronouncement
___22. TACTILE   V. Described
___23. CADENCED   W. Humiliating failure; a fall on the buttocks
___24. ERECTED   X. Returning like for like, especially evil
___25. MELANCHOLY   Y. Sadness; gloominess

Fahrenheit 451 Vocabulary Matching 4 Answer Key

Q - 1. PYRE	A.	Reduced to powder
E - 2. PROCLIVITIES	B.	Showed; revealed
T - 3. ODIOUS	C.	Not able to make a decision
U - 4. DICTUM	D.	Wordiness
L - 5. CARDAMON	E.	Predispositions; tendencies
G - 6. SMOLDERING	F.	Not readily noticed or seen; not commonly known
V - 7. LIMNED	G.	Burning with little smoke and no flame
A - 8. PULVERIZED	H.	Deflected; avoided
N - 9. STOLID	I.	The study of the dynamics of projectiles
O -10. MULTIFACETED	J.	Overwhelming, advancing sight crushing all in its path
C -11. INDECISIVE	K.	Relating to the sense of touch
S -12. PEDANTS	L.	Indian Spice
P -13. RAVENOUS	M.	With a rhythmic flow
W -14. PRATFALL	N.	Having or revealing little emotion
F -15. OBSCURE	O.	Having many faces
B -16. MANIFESTED	P.	Extremely hungry; greedy for gratification
D -17. VERBIAGE	Q.	A pile of combustible materials for burning a corpse
X -18. RETALIATION	R.	Set up; established
I - 19. BALLISTICS	S.	Those who flaunt their knowledge
J - 20. JUGGERNAUT	T.	Arousing strong dislike or displeasure
H -21. PARRIED	U.	Authoritative pronouncement
K -22. TACTILE	V.	Described
M -23. CADENCED	W.	Humiliating failure; a fall on the buttocks
R -24. ERECTED	X.	Returning like for like, especially evil
Y -25. MELANCHOLY	Y.	Sadness; gloominess

Fahrenheit 451 Vocabulary Magic Squares 1

Match the definition with the vocabulary word. Put your answers in the magic squares below. When your answers are correct, all columns and rows will add to the same number.

A. RECEPTACLE   G. GROTESQUE   M. REFRACTED
B. ODIOUS   H. RAVENOUS   N. COWARDICE
C. CARDAMON   I. CAPILLARY   O. STOLID
D. PRATFALL   J. INDECISIVE   P. PROCLIVITIES
E. MANIFESTED   K. PARRIED
F. LIMNED   L. SMOLDERING

1. Indian Spice
2. Not able to make a decision
3. Described
4. Having or revealing little emotion
5. Predispositions; tendencies
6. Showed; revealed
7. Fine; small in diameter
8. Humiliating failure; a fall on the buttocks
9. Deflected from a straight path
10. Extremely hungry; greedy for gratification
11. Burning with little smoke and no flame
12. A container that holds matter
13. Arousing strong dislike or displeasure
14. Deflected; avoided
15. Bizarre; distorted
16. Lacks courage in the face of danger

A = 12	B = 13	C = 1	D = 8
E = 6	F = 3	G = 15	H = 10
I = 7	J = 2	K = 14	L = 11
M = 9	N = 16	O = 4	P = 5

Fahrenheit 451 Vocabulary Magic Squares 1 Answer Key

Match the definition with the vocabulary word. Put your answers in the magic squares below. When your answers are correct, all columns and rows will add to the same number.

A. RECEPTACLE
B. ODIOUS
C. CARDAMON
D. PRATFALL
E. MANIFESTED
F. LIMNED
G. GROTESQUE
H. RAVENOUS
I. CAPILLARY
J. INDECISIVE
K. PARRIED
L. SMOLDERING
M. REFRACTED
N. COWARDICE
O. STOLID
P. PROCLIVITIES

1. Indian Spice
2. Not able to make a decision
3. Described
4. Having or revealing little emotion
5. Predispositions; tendencies
6. Showed; revealed
7. Fine; small in diameter
8. Humiliating failure; a fall on the buttocks
9. Deflected from a straight path
10. Extremely hungry; greedy for gratification
11. Burning with little smoke and no flame
12. A container that holds matter
13. Arousing strong dislike or displeasure
14. Deflected; avoided
15. Bizarre; distorted
16. Lacks courage in the face of danger

A=12	B=13	C=1	D=8
E=6	F=3	G=15	H=10
I=7	J=2	K=14	L=11
M=9	N=16	O=4	P=5

Fahrenheit 451 Vocabulary Magic Squares 2

Match the definition with the vocabulary word. Put your answers in the magic squares below. When your answers are correct, all columns and rows will add to the same number.

A. COWARDICE
B. ERECTED
C. BALLISTICS
D. CENTRIFUGE
E. SMOLDERING
F. LIMNED
G. CARDAMON
H. PULVERIZED
I. ODIOUS
J. JUGGERNAUT
K. TACTILE
L. PEDANTS
M. REFRACTED
N. GROTESQUE
O. DICTUM
P. PRATFALL

1. Reduced to powder
2. Deflected from a straight path
3. Set up; established
4. Relating to the sense of touch
5. Overwhelming, advancing sight crushing all in its path
6. The study of the dynamics of projectiles
7. Humiliating failure; a fall on the buttocks
8. Burning with little smoke and no flame
9. Authoritative pronouncement
10. Described
11. Arousing strong dislike or displeasure
12. Apparatus consisting of a compartment spun around a central axis
13. Lack courage in the face of danger
14. Those who flaunt their knowledge
15. Indian Spice
16. Bizarre; distorted

A=	B=	C=	D=
E=	F=	G=	H=
I=	J=	K=	L=
M=	N=	O=	P=

Fahrenheit 451 Vocabulary Magic Squares 2 Answer Key

Match the definition with the vocabulary word. Put your answers in the magic squares below. When your answers are correct, all columns and rows will add to the same number.

A. COWARDICE
B. ERECTED
C. BALLISTICS
D. CENTRIFUGE
E. SMOLDERING
F. LIMNED
G. CARDAMON
H. PULVERIZED
I. ODIOUS
J. JUGGERNAUT
K. TACTILE
L. PEDANTS
M. REFRACTED
N. GROTESQUE
O. DICTUM
P. PRATFALL

1. Reduced to powder
2. Deflected from a straight path
3. Set up; established
4. Relating to the sense of touch
5. Overwhelming, advancing sight crushing all in its path
6. The study of the dynamics of projectiles
7. Humiliating failure; a fall on the buttocks
8. Burning with little smoke and no flame
9. Authoritative pronouncement
10. Described
11. Arousing strong dislike or displeasure
12. Apparatus consisting of a compartment spun around a central axis
13. Lacks courage in the face of danger
14. Those who flaunt their knowledge
15. Indian Spice
16. Bizarre; distorted

A=13	B=3	C=6	D=12
E=8	F=10	G=15	H=1
I=11	J=5	K=4	L=14
M=2	N=16	O=9	P=7

Fahrenheit 451 Vocabulary Magic Squares 3

Match the definition with the vocabulary word. Put your answers in the magic squares below. When your answers are correct, all columns and rows will add to the same number.

A. BALLISTICS
B. CENTRIFUGE
C. COWARDICE
D. INDECISIVE
E. ODIOUS
F. VERBIAGE
G. RECEPTACLE
H. REFRACTED
I. LIMNED
J. CADENCED
K. CAPILLARY
L. PARRIED
M. IMPERCEPTIBLY
N. STOLID
O. ERECTED
P. OBSCURE

1. Having or revealing little emotion
2. A container that holds matter
3. Deflected; avoided
4. The study of the dynamics of projectiles
5. Fine; small in diameter
6. Apparatus consisting of a compartment spun around a central axis
7. Impossible to detect by ordinary senses
8. Deflected from a straight path
9. Arousing strong dislike or displeasure
10. Not readily noticed or seen; not commonly known
11. Lacks courage in the face of danger
12. With a rhythmic flow
13. Not able to make a decision
14. Described
15. Wordiness
16. Set up; established

A= 4	B= 6	C= 11	D= 13
E= 9	F= 15	G= 2	H= 8
I= 14	J= 12	K= 5	L= 3
M= 7	N= 1	O= 16	P= 10

Fahrenheit 451 Vocabulary Magic Squares 3 Answer Key

Match the definition with the vocabulary word. Put your answers in the magic squares below. When your answers are correct, all columns and rows will add to the same number.

A. BALLISTICS
B. CENTRIFUGE
C. COWARDICE
D. INDECISIVE
E. ODIOUS
F. VERBIAGE
G. RECEPTACLE
H. REFRACTED
I. LIMNED
J. CADENCED
K. CAPILLARY
L. PARRIED
M. IMPERCEPTIBLY
N. STOLID
O. ERECTED
P. OBSCURE

1. Having or revealing little emotion
2. A container that holds matter
3. Deflected; avoided
4. The study of the dynamics of projectiles
5. Fine; small in diameter
6. Apparatus consisting of a compartment spun around a central axis
7. Impossible to detect by ordinary senses
8. Deflected from a straight path
9. Arousing strong dislike or displeasure
10. Not readily noticed or seen; not commonly known
11. Lacks courage in the face of danger
12. With a rhythmic flow
13. Not able to make a decision
14. Described
15. Wordiness
16. Set up; established

A=4	B=6	C=11	D=13
E=9	F=15	G=2	H=8
I=14	J=12	K=5	L=3
M=7	N=1	O=16	P=10

Fahrenheit 451 Vocabulary Magic Squares 4

Match the definition with the vocabulary word. Put your answers in the magic squares below. When your answers are correct, all columns and rows will add to the same number.

A. IMPERCEPTIBLY
B. STOLID
C. MELANCHOLY
D. REFRACTED
E. RAVENOUS
F. CADENCED
G. VERBIAGE
H. ODIOUS
I. OBSCURE
J. JUGGERNAUT
K. TACTILE
L. PARRIED
M. RETALIATION
N. ERECTED
O. NONCOMBUSTIBLE
P. MANIFESTED

1. Having or revealing little emotion
2. Wordiness
3. Relating to the sense of touch
4. Set up; established
5. Returning like for like, especially evil
6. Deflected; avoided
7. Arousing strong dislike or displeasure
8. Impossible to detect by ordinary senses
9. Showed; revealed
10. Not readily noticed or seen; not commonly known
11. Extremely hungry; greedy for gratification
12. Deflected from a straight path
13. Sadness; gloominess
14. With a rhythmic flow
15. Overwhelming, advancing sight crushing all in its path
16. Does not burn easily

A=	B=	C=	D=
E=	F=	G=	H=
I=	J=	K=	L=
M=	N=	O=	P=

Fahrenheit 451 Vocabulary Magic Squares 4 Answer Key

Match the definition with the vocabulary word. Put your answers in the magic squares below. When your answers are correct, all columns and rows will add to the same number.

A. IMPERCEPTIBLY
B. STOLID
C. MELANCHOLY
D. REFRACTED
E. RAVENOUS
F. CADENCED
G. VERBIAGE
H. ODIOUS
I. OBSCURE
J. JUGGERNAUT
K. TACTILE
L. PARRIED
M. RETALIATION
N. ERECTED
O. NONCOMBUSTIBLE
P. MANIFESTED

1. Having or revealing little emotion
2. Wordiness
3. Relating to the sense of touch
4. Set up; established
5. Returning like for like, especially evil
6. Deflected; avoided
7. Arousing strong dislike or displeasure
8. Impossible to detect by ordinary senses
9. Showed; revealed
10. Not readily noticed or seen; not commonly known
11. Extremely hungry; greedy for gratification
12. Deflected from a straight path
13. Sadness; gloominess
14. With a rhythmic flow
15. Overwhelming, advancing sight crushing all in its path
16. Does not burn easily

A=8	B=1	C=13	D=12
E=11	F=14	G=2	H=7
I=10	J=15	K=3	L=6
M=5	N=4	O=16	P=9

Fahrenheit 451 Vocabulary Word Search 1

```
P N O N C O M B U S T I B L E M C N I R
R U Y Z Z J L R T H F N W T M O O C M G
K S L M T U A N R E G G U J W I B A P J
S Y O V G Q A B H T S D Q A T X H D E R
H M H G E D P N O M A D R A C D Y E R T
N X C K E R H X Z Y R D I Q N R H N C S
Y N N P Y Q I W T L I L B J A E V C E Z
M W A W R B M Z X C A Y K L V C Z E P D
G Y L T S E P P E T Z K L H E E M D T J
D F E D C Z F M E D P I E F R P A P I X
E R M F I J L R L R P R R W B T N P B X
I G V W T B H M A A F B E J I A I K L V
R W B G S S N T C C C B C X A C F Y Y T
R B J V I K F O P F T M T W G L E C D L
A H V H L A P J D S J E E F E E S E N Z
P R O C L I V I T I E S D T A C T I L E
X B P L A Y L O N Y O C C J B E E P R R
D R V C B R L D Y W B U L K C N D D A W
F R W J K I E D T G X H S A W T E V V Q
H P D J D C B Q I F S D F C P R H P E Z
D M H F I X C C M C E I T Z U I Y R N M
Q M F S M H N N G N T M J C T F C S O F
S Q I W G G F F M L V U S T H U M Y U J
B V P Y R E V I U H Q B M H D G M G S V
E W C Y F G L M L R O G R O T E S Q U E
```

A container that holds matter (10)
A pile of combustible materials for burning a corpse (4)
Apparatus consisting of a compartment spun around a central axis (10)
Arousing strong dislike or displeasure (6)
Authoritative pronouncement (6)
Bizarre; distorted (9)
Deflected from a straight path (9)
Deflected; avoided (7)
Described (6)
Does not burn easily (14)
Extremely hungry; greedy for gratification (8)
Fine; small in diameter (9)
Having many faces (12)
Having or revealing little emotion (6)
Humiliating failure; a fall on the buttocks (8)
Lacks courage in the face of danger (9)
Impossible to detect by ordinary senses (13)
Indian Spice (8)
Not able to make a decision (10)
Not readily noticed or seen; not commonly known (7)

Overwhelming, advancing sight crushing all in its path (10)
Predispositions; tendencies (12)
Reduced to powder (10)
Relating to the sense of touch (7)
Returning like for like, especially evil (11)
Sadness; gloominess (10)
Set up; established (7)
Showed; revealed (10)
The study of the dynamics of projectiles (10)
Those who flaunt their knowledge (7)
With a rhythmic flow (8)
Wordiness (8)

Fahrenheit 451 Vocabulary Word Search 1 Answer Key

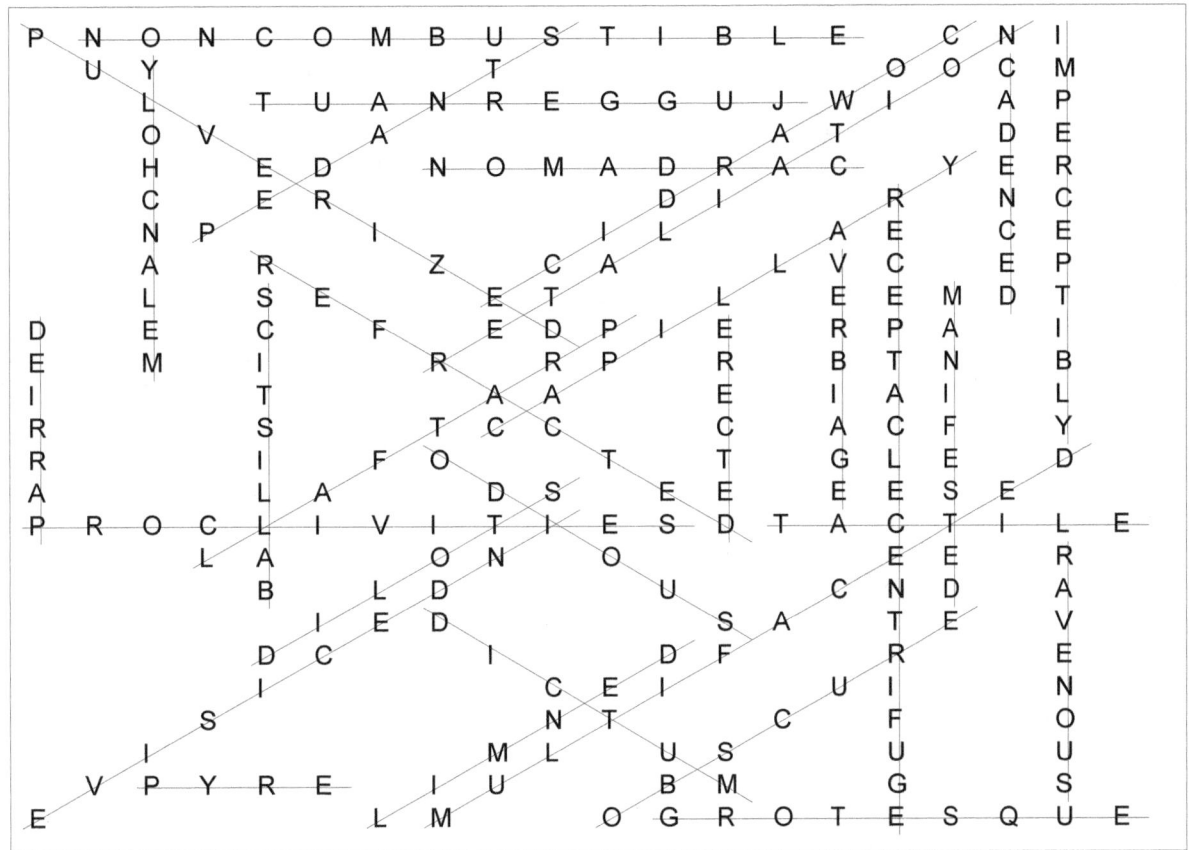

A container that holds matter (10)
A pile of combustible materials for burning a corpse (4)
Apparatus consisting of a compartment spun around a central axis (10)
Arousing strong dislike or displeasure (6)
Authoritative pronouncement (6)
Bizarre; distorted (9)
Deflected from a straight path (9)
Deflected; avoided (7)
Described (6)
Does not burn easily (14)
Extremely hungry; greedy for gratification (8)
Fine; small in diameter (9)
Having many faces (12)
Having or revealing little emotion (6)
Humiliating failure; a fall on the buttocks (8)
Lacks courage in the face of danger (9)
Impossible to detect by ordinary senses (13)
Indian Spice (8)
Not able to make a decision (10)
Not readily noticed or seen; not commonly known (7)
Overwhelming, advancing sight crushing all in its path (10)
Predispositions; tendencies (12)
Reduced to powder (10)
Relating to the sense of touch (7)
Returning like for like, especially evil (11)
Sadness; gloominess (10)
Set up; established (7)
Showed; revealed (10)
The study of the dynamics of projectiles (10)
Those who flaunt their knowledge (7)
With a rhythmic flow (8)
Wordiness (8)

Fahrenheit 451 Vocabulary Word Search 2

```
R E F R A C T E D C O W A R D I C E P Z
S E P C S K Z Q B X S V V V R C N D R T
I G C Y W G P M A N I F E S T E D E A P
M L P E Y R A L L I P A C J W N L Z T K
U D R D P O K D F F D H J V K T P I F Y
L C O K M T H Q H K F F B M J R C R A G
T L C L U E A J I N D E C I S I V E L D
A M L W L S T C K F Z F F K V F T V L D
N P I X T Q Q Y L S M V W S B U J L J K
E R V P I U Z R W E M M K A T G L U S J
O E I B F E S N Y X M O L N P E G P Y L
U T T S A L R Z L S P L L Q C G W Y Q B
S A I T C C V Z B M I E H D E S B L N R
L L E G E J D C I S J T D R E T W O X G
Y I S L T F B Q T S P H N A K R M H N Y
R A S L E Q M I P D G A L Q N A I C K W
D T L B D S C F E E U V R E D T M N E Q
D I L O T S T A C T I L E R Y P S A G Z
K O C N V D N Z R C O G A U I V Y L A D
K N T T E G R W E E D C N C T E S E I X
G R N N U Z C W P R I K G S Z T D M B K
T X M H M M X Q M E O N Y B H W Z C R R
X I T L R H G L I D U D N O Q M X X E D
L C A D E N C E D V S U O N E V A R V B
N O N C O M B U S T I B L E V L F P X P
```

A container that holds matter (10)
A pile of combustible materials for burning a corpse (4)
Apparatus consisting of a compartment spun around a central axis (10)
Arousing strong dislike or displeasure (6)
Authoritative pronouncement (6)
Bizarre; distorted (9)
Burning with little smoke and no flame (10)
Deflected from a straight path (9)
Deflected; avoided (7)
Described (6)
Does not burn easily (14)
Extremely hungry; greedy for gratification (8)
Fine; small in diameter (9)
Happening at the same time (14)
Having many faces (12)
Having or revealing little emotion (6)
Humiliating failure; a fall on the buttocks (8)
Lacks courage in the face of danger (9)
Impossible to detect by ordinary senses (13)
Indian Spice (8)
Not able to make a decision (10)

Not readily noticed or seen; not commonly known (7)
Overwhelming, advancing sight crushing all in its path (10)
Predispositions; tendencies (12)
Reduced to powder (10)
Relating to the sense of touch (7)
Returning like for like, especially evil (11)
Sadness; gloominess (10)
Set up; established (7)
Showed; revealed (10)
The study of the dynamics of projectiles (10)
Those who flaunt their knowledge (7)
With a rhythmic flow (8)
Wordiness (8)

Fahrenheit 451 Vocabulary Word Search 2 Answer Key

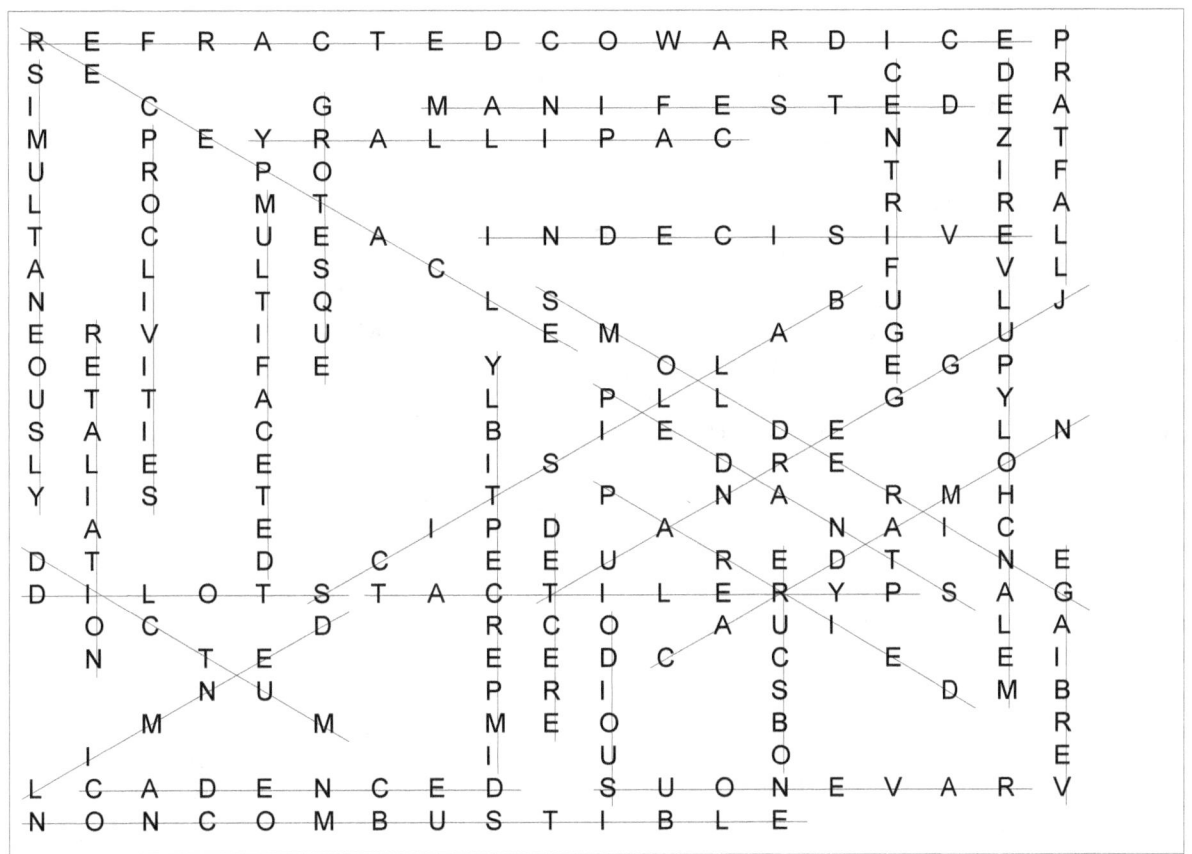

A container that holds matter (10)
A pile of combustible materials for burning a corpse (4)
Apparatus consisting of a compartment spun around a central axis (10)
Arousing strong dislike or displeasure (6)
Authoritative pronouncement (6)
Bizarre; distorted (9)
Burning with little smoke and no flame (10)
Deflected from a straight path (9)
Deflected; avoided (7)
Described (6)
Does not burn easily (14)
Extremely hungry; greedy for gratification (8)
Fine; small in diameter (9)
Happening at the same time (14)
Having many faces (12)
Having or revealing little emotion (6)
Humiliating failure; a fall on the buttocks (8)
Lacks courage in the face of danger (9)
Impossible to detect by ordinary senses (13)
Indian Spice (8)
Not able to make a decision (10)

Not readily noticed or seen; not commonly known (7)
Overwhelming, advancing sight crushing all in its path (10)
Predispositions; tendencies (12)
Reduced to powder (10)
Relating to the sense of touch (7)
Returning like for like, especially evil (11)
Sadness; gloominess (10)
Set up; established (7)
Showed; revealed (10)
The study of the dynamics of projectiles (10)
Those who flaunt their knowledge (7)
With a rhythmic flow (8)
Wordiness (8)

Fahrenheit 451 Vocabulary Word Search 3

```
R E F R A C T E D C O W A R D I C E P J
S E V F L L X F H W Z X H F H C V D R B
I T C W Z G G M A N I F E S T E D E A C
M C P E Y R A L L I P A C S X N B Z T T
U V R H P O P P Q H S Q G M Y T M I F L
L F O T M T F G H S B P P F C R B R A F
T Q C F U E A K I N D E C I S I V E L C
A W L Y L S C C L C D V C V R F Z V L Q
N M I F T Q T H L S H L Q S B U S L J B
E R V X I U Y Y P E M L K A N G B U H N
O E I C F E G M Y X J O L H G E G P K H
U T T V A B R N L M P L L W V G J Y C N
S A I Y C J M K B V I E D D E R H L N G
L L E R E C R L I S Y J D R E Y F O S Y
Y I S R T G F L T W P X N A W R M H C B
J A W T E W K I P D T A M Q N A I C J L
D T H Y D L C G E E U Z R E D T L N E D
D I L O T S T A C T I L E R Y P S A G Q
C O C T Y D K X R C O F A U I P D L A P
W N B T E N G H E E D C N C S E Y E I Y
G S X N U M M X P R I Z K S G R D M B W
C G M H J M T Q M E O G Q B X X J V R G
H I W G F K Y K I K U T T O L W Y G E X
L C A D E N C E D P S U O N E V A R V H
N O N C O M B U S T I B L E Q Y W M C Z
```

BALLISTICS	IMPERCEPTIBLY	ODIOUS	REFRACTED
CADENCED	INDECISIVE	PARRIED	RETALIATION
CAPILLARY	JUGGERNAUT	PEDANTS	SIMULTANEOUSLY
CARDAMON	LIMNED	PRATFALL	SMOLDERING
CENTRIFUGE	MANIFESTED	PROCLIVITIES	STOLID
COWARDICE	MELANCHOLY	PULVERIZED	TACTILE
DICTUM	MULTIFACETED	PYRE	VERBIAGE
ERECTED	NONCOMBUSTIBLE	RAVENOUS	
GROTESQUE	OBSCURE	RECEPTACLE	

Fahrenheit 451 Vocabulary Word Search 3 Answer Key

BALLISTICS	IMPERCEPTIBLY	ODIOUS	REFRACTED
CADENCED	INDECISIVE	PARRIED	RETALIATION
CAPILLARY	JUGGERNAUT	PEDANTS	SIMULTANEOUSLY
CARDAMON	LIMNED	PRATFALL	SMOLDERING
CENTRIFUGE	MANIFESTED	PROCLIVITIES	STOLID
COWARDICE	MELANCHOLY	PULVERIZED	TACTILE
DICTUM	MULTIFACETED	PYRE	VERBIAGE
ERECTED	NONCOMBUSTIBLE	RAVENOUS	
GROTESQUE	OBSCURE	RECEPTACLE	

Fahrenheit 451 Vocabulary Word Search 4

```
V M E L A N C H O L Y B V G S Y J K D K
P E Q Q E S C S Q X G A W J R H Q I P K
K C R Z L J M K F M V L D W V V L M X B
M A J B B R P G P P S L H G C O T P P S
A P U V I D N O I T A I L A T E R E Y D
N I G C T A C N R P S S D S S V G R M B
I L G R S R G H X U B T Z T M H S C U F
F L E S U N T E S L V I D D B N N E L H
E A R F B D C F M V Z C W R E N S P T D
S R N T M H X J O E Y S F H U Y C T I J
T Y A M O N S X L R E L P M Q F W I F R
E S U W C T T Q D I V P P W S H K B A K
D U T C N T K L E Z I J H P E P Y L C Z
Q O M A O S L S R E S K R Y T C Y Y E W
R N D K N A V V I D I O Y E O C W R T D
F E G U F I R T N E C O W A R D I C E G
P V C T K P W M G L E B G K G E A T D B
R A A E Q V L M I I D S H V J D C H C V
P R P N P Z X V T T N C Y Z E A C T G D
P A K C F T I M G C I U V N R S M K E L
X W R B X T A X M A G R C F U U K N S D
W P X R I X S C Z T C E E O T T M T K N
J M P E I N G J L D D R I C W I X Y H F
F Z S T P E P M F E R D I V L H T V V S
S G N O M A D R A C O D T L H B W K K K
```

BALLISTICS	IMPERCEPTIBLY	ODIOUS	REFRACTED
CADENCED	INDECISIVE	PARRIED	RETALIATION
CAPILLARY	JUGGERNAUT	PEDANTS	SMOLDERING
CARDAMON	LIMNED	PRATFALL	STOLID
CENTRIFUGE	MANIFESTED	PROCLIVITIES	TACTILE
COWARDICE	MELANCHOLY	PULVERIZED	VERBIAGE
DICTUM	MULTIFACETED	PYRE	
ERECTED	NONCOMBUSTIBLE	RAVENOUS	
GROTESQUE	OBSCURE	RECEPTACLE	

Fahrenheit 451 Vocabulary Word Search 4 Answer Key

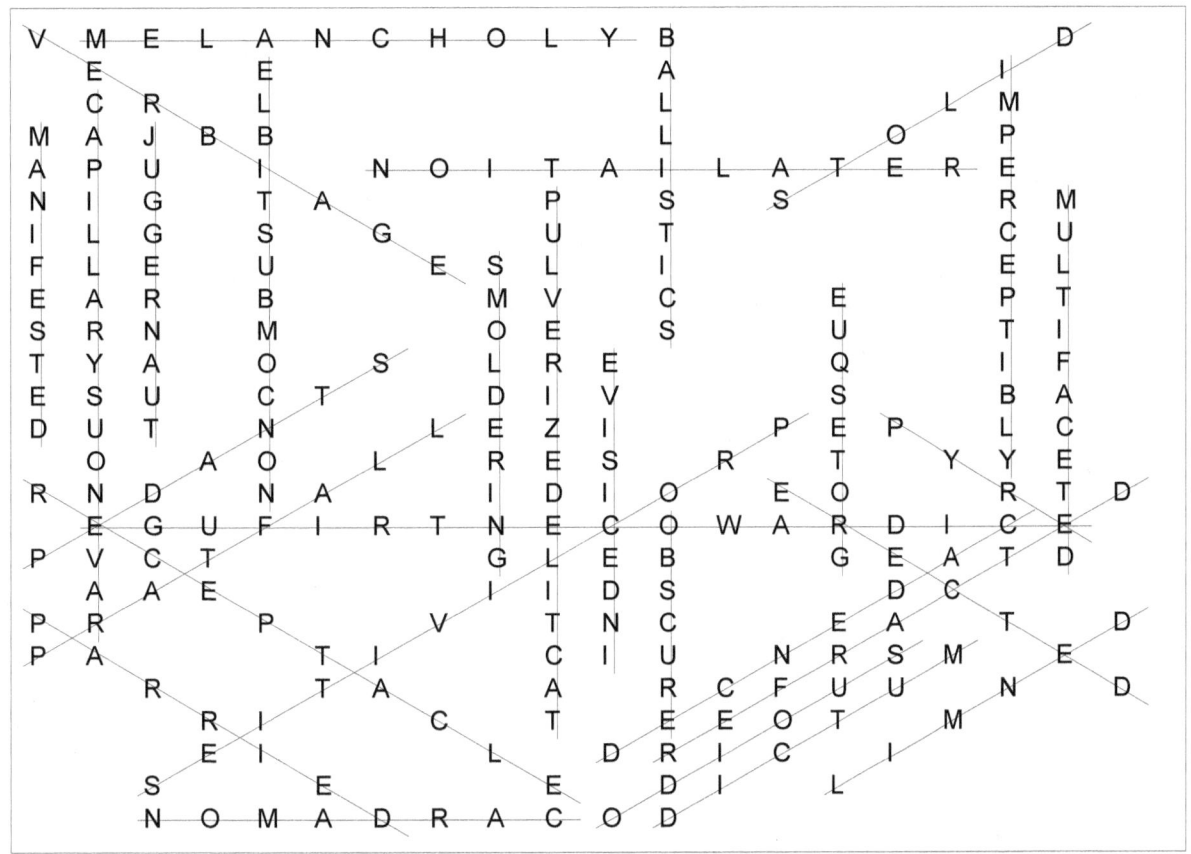

BALLISTICS	IMPERCEPTIBLY	ODIOUS	REFRACTED
CADENCED	INDECISIVE	PARRIED	RETALIATION
CAPILLARY	JUGGERNAUT	PEDANTS	SMOLDERING
CARDAMON	LIMNED	PRATFALL	STOLID
CENTRIFUGE	MANIFESTED	PROCLIVITIES	TACTILE
COWARDICE	MELANCHOLY	PULVERIZED	VERBIAGE
DICTUM	MULTIFACETED	PYRE	
ERECTED	NONCOMBUSTIBLE	RAVENOUS	
GROTESQUE	OBSCURE	RECEPTACLE	

Fahrenheit 451 Vocabulary Crossword 1

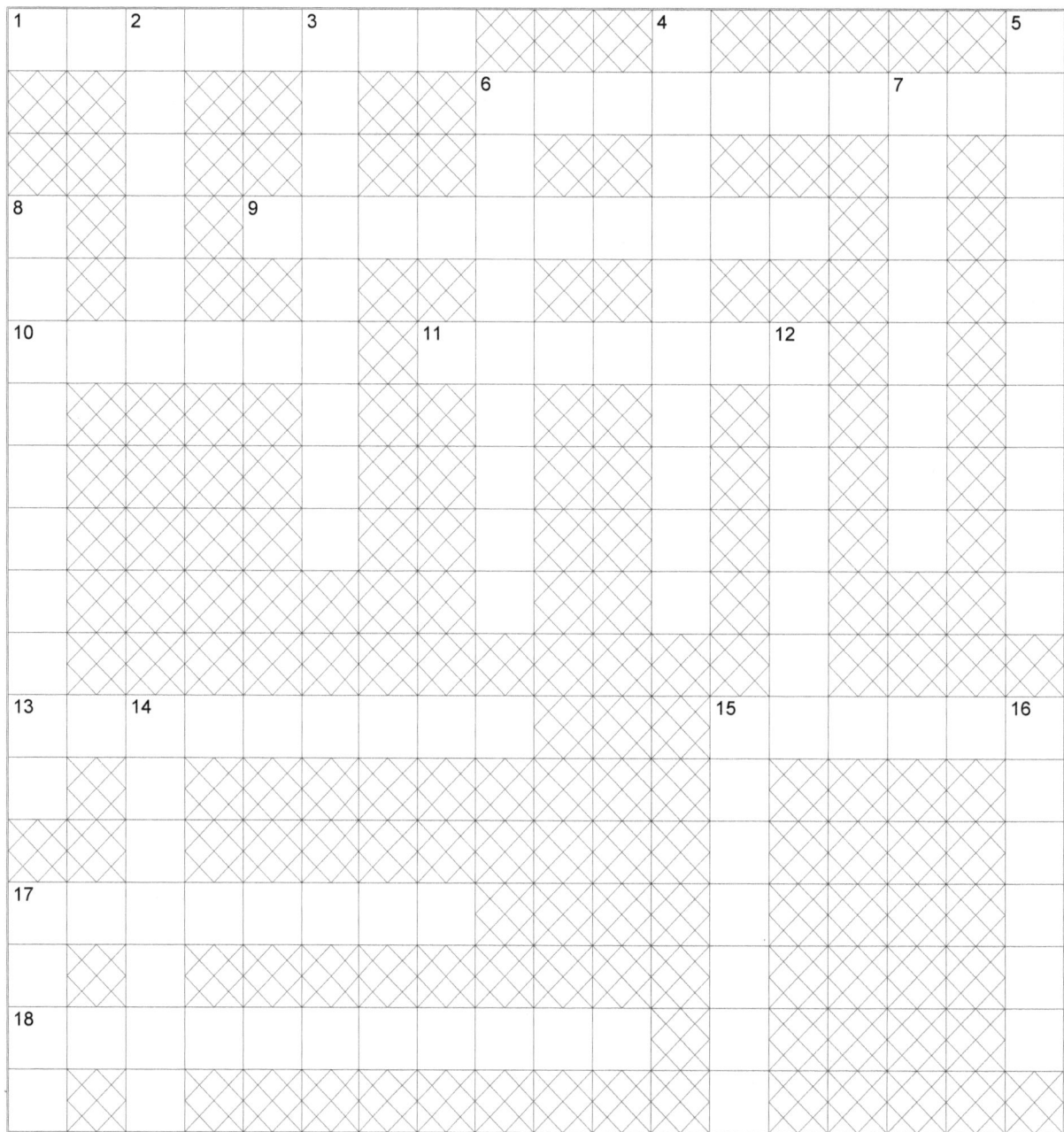

Across
1. With a rhythmic flow
6. A container that holds matter
9. Showed; revealed
10. Described
11. Relating to the sense of touch
13. Fine; small in diameter
15. Arousing strong dislike or displeasure
17. Humiliating failure; a fall on the buttocks
18. Returning like for like, especially evil

Down
2. Authoritative pronouncement
3. Lacks courage in the face of danger
4. Apparatus consisting of a compartment spun around a central axis
5. Sadness; gloominess
6. Deflected from a straight path
7. Indian Spice
8. The study of the dynamics of projectiles
12. Set up; established
14. Those who flaunt their knowledge
15. Not readily noticed or seen; not commonly known
16. Having or revealing little emotion
17. A pile of combustible materials for burning a corpse

Fahrenheit 451 Vocabulary Crossword 1 Answer Key

	1 C	2 A	D	E	3 N	C	E	D		4 C			5 M
		I			O		6 R	E	C	E	P	7 T	A	C	L	E
		C			W		E			N			A			L
8 B		T		9 M	A	N	I	F	E	S	T	E	D			A
A		U		R			R			R			D			N
10 L	I	M	N	E	D		11 T	A	C	T	I	L	12 E			C
L				I			C			F			R		M		H
I				C			T			U			E		O		O
S				E			E			G			C		N		L
T							D			E			T			Y
I													E			
13 C	A	14 P	I	L	L	A	R	Y		15 O	D	I	O	U	S	16 S
		S		E						B						T
		E		D						S						O
17 P	R	A	T	F	A	L	L			C						L
Y		N								U						I
18 R	E	T	A	L	I	A	T	I	O	N		R				D
E		S								R						

Across
1. With a rhythmic flow
6. A container that holds matter
9. Showed; revealed
10. Described
11. Relating to the sense of touch
13. Fine; small in diameter
15. Arousing strong dislike or displeasure
17. Humiliating failure; a fall on the buttocks
18. Returning like for like, especially evil

Down
2. Authoritative pronouncement
3. Lacks courage in the face of danger
4. Apparatus consisting of a compartment spun around a central axis
5. Sadness; gloominess
6. Deflected from a straight path
7. Indian Spice
8. The study of the dynamics of projectiles
12. Set up; established
14. Those who flaunt their knowledge
15. Not readily noticed or seen; not commonly known
16. Having or revealing little emotion
17. A pile of combustible materials for burning a corpse

Fahrenheit 451 Vocabulary Crossword 2

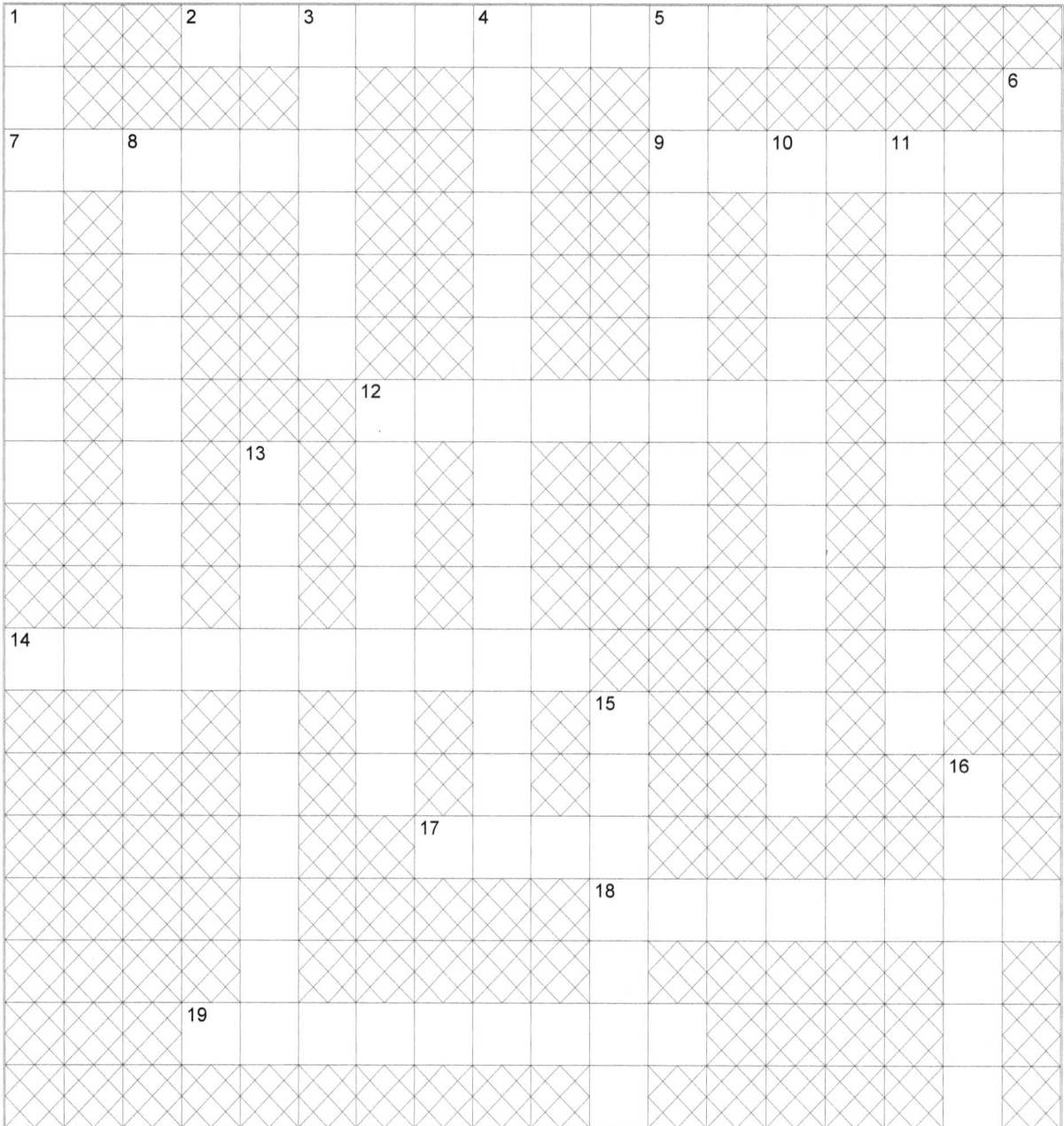

Across
2. The study of the dynamics of projectiles
7. Authoritative pronouncement
9. Deflected; avoided
12. Humiliating failure; a fall on the buttocks
14. Overwhelming, advancing sight crushing all in its path
17. A pile of combustible materials for burning a corpse
18. Indian Spice
19. Deflected from a straight path

Down
1. With a rhythmic flow
3. Described
4. Happening at the same time
5. Fine; small in diameter
6. Arousing strong dislike or displeasure
8. Apparatus consisting of a compartment spun around a central axis
10. Returning like for like, especially evil
11. Not able to make a decision
12. Those who flaunt their knowledge
13. A container that holds matter
15. Set up; established
16. Having or revealing little emotion

Fahrenheit 451 Vocabulary Crossword 2 Answer Key

	1 C		2 B	3 A	L	L	4 I	S	T	I	5 C	S		
	A			I			I				A			6 O
7 D	I	8 C	T	U	M		M		9 P	10 A	R	11 R	I	E	D
	E		E		N		U		I		E		N		I
	N		N		E		L		L		T		D		O
	C		T		D		T		L		A		E		U
	E		R			12 P	R	A	T	F	A	L	L		C	S
	D		I		13 R	E		N		A		L		I	
			F		E		D		E		R		I		A		S
			U		C		A		O		Y		A		S	
14 J	U	G	G	E	R	N	A	U	T				T		I	
			E		P		T		S		15 E				O		E
					T		S			L		R				N		16 S
					A				17 P	Y	R	E						T
					C							18 C	A	R	D	A	M	O	N
					L							T						L
				19 R	E	F	R	A	C	T	E	D					I
												D					D

Across
2. The study of the dynamics of projectiles
7. Authoritative pronouncement
9. Deflected; avoided
12. Humiliating failure; a fall on the buttocks
14. Overwhelming, advancing sight crushing all in its path
17. A pile of combustible materials for burning a corpse
18. Indian Spice
19. Deflected from a straight path

Down
1. With a rhythmic flow
3. Described
4. Happening at the same time
5. Fine; small in diameter
6. Arousing strong dislike or displeasure
8. Apparatus consisting of a compartment spun around a central axis
10. Returning like for like, especially evil
11. Not able to make a decision
12. Those who flaunt their knowledge
13. A container that holds matter
15. Set up; established
16. Having or revealing little emotion

Fahrenheit 451 Vocabulary Crossword 3

Across
1. Those who flaunt their knowledge
5. Does not burn easily
8. Predispositions; tendencies
10. Returning like for like, especially evil
13. A pile of combustible materials for burning a corpse
14. Humiliating failure; a fall on the buttocks
16. Fine; small in diameter
17. Set up; established

Down
2. Authoritative pronouncement
3. The study of the dynamics of projectiles
4. Having or revealing little emotion
6. Not readily noticed or seen; not commonly known
7. Happening at the same time
8. Deflected; avoided
9. Burning with little smoke and no flame
10. A container that holds matter
11. Arousing strong dislike or displeasure
12. Relating to the sense of touch
15. Described

Fahrenheit 451 Vocabulary Crossword 3 Answer Key

	1 P	2 E	D	A	N	T	S		3 B			
		I					4 S		A			
5 N	6 O	N	C	O	M	B	U	S	T	I	B	L	E	
	B		T				O		L		7 S	
	S		U	8 P	R	O	C	L	I	V	I	T	I	E	9 S
	C		M	A			I		S		M		M
	U			R			D		T		U		O
	R			R			I		I		L		L
10 R	E	T	A	L	I	A	T	I	11 O	N		C		T		D
E				E			D		S		A		E
C				D			I			N		R
E		12 T					O		13 P	Y	R	E		I
14 P	R	A	T	F	15 A	L	L		U				O		N
T		C			I				S				U		G
A		T			M								S
C		I			N		16 C	A	P	I	L	L	A	R	Y
L		L			E							Y
17 E	R	E	C	T	E	D

Across
1. Those who flaunt their knowledge
5. Does not burn easily
8. Predispositions; tendencies
10. Returning like for like, especially evil
13. A pile of combustible materials for burning a corpse
14. Humiliating failure; a fall on the buttocks
16. Fine; small in diameter
17. Set up; established

Down
2. Authoritative pronouncement
3. The study of the dynamics of projectiles
4. Having or revealing little emotion
6. Not readily noticed or seen; not commonly known
7. Happening at the same time
8. Deflected; avoided
9. Burning with little smoke and no flame
10. A container that holds matter
11. Arousing strong dislike or displeasure
12. Relating to the sense of touch
15. Described

Fahrenheit 451 Vocabulary Crossword 4

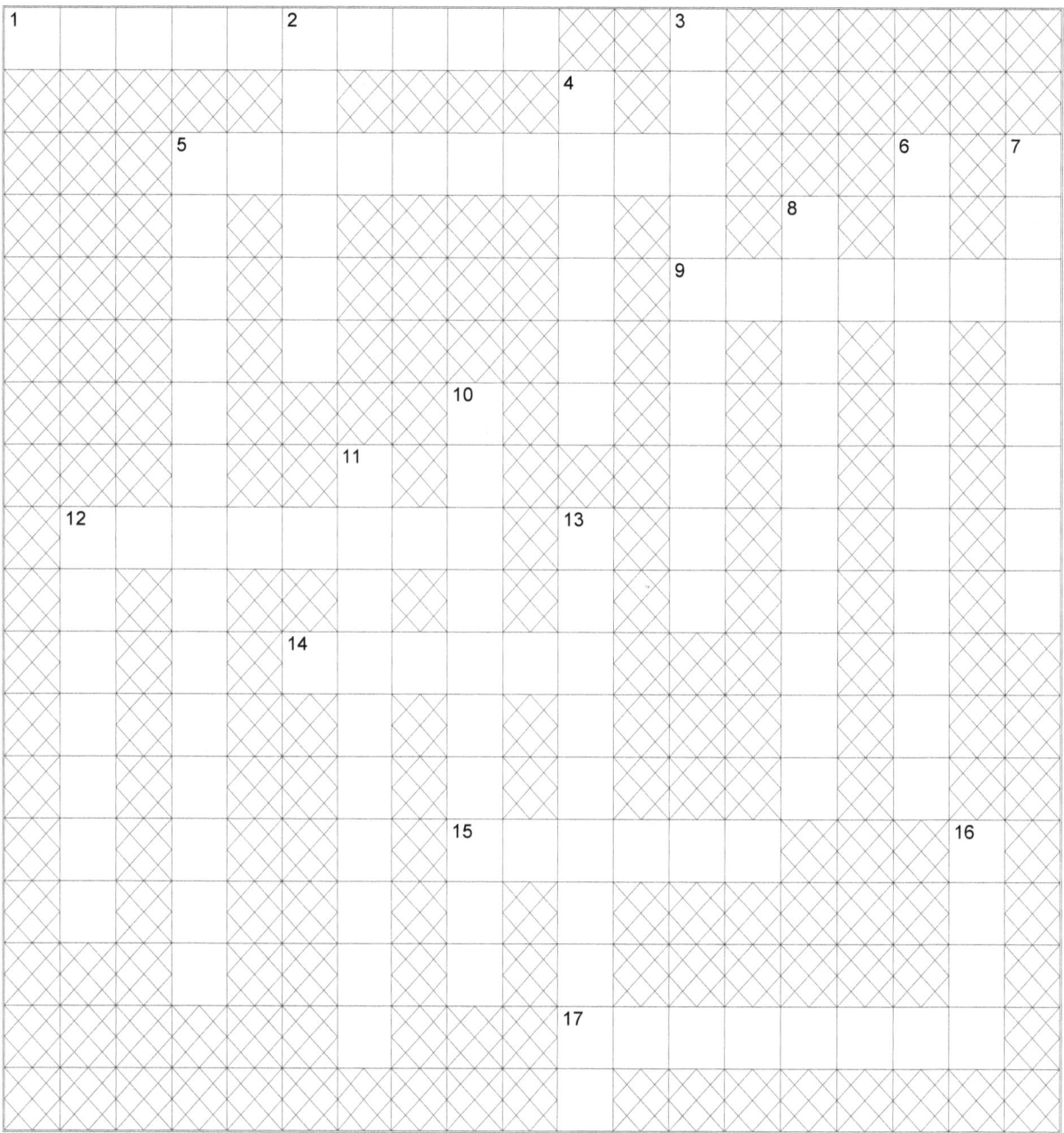

Across
1. The study of the dynamics of projectiles
5. Burning with little smoke and no flame
9. Set up; established
12. Humiliating failure; a fall on the buttocks
14. Described
15. Arousing strong dislike or displeasure
17. Wordiness

Down
2. Having or revealing little emotion
3. Overwhelming, advancing sight crushing all in its path
4. Authoritative pronouncement
5. Happening at the same time
6. Returning like for like, especially evil
7. With a rhythmic flow
8. Apparatus consisting of a compartment spun around a central axis
10. Sadness; gloominess
11. Showed; revealed
12. Those who flaunt their knowledge
13. Not able to make a decision
16. A pile of combustible materials for burning a corpse

Fahrenheit 451 Vocabulary Crossword 4 Answer Key

	1 B	A	L	L	2 I S	T	I	C	S		3 J			
					T				4 D		U			
			5 S	M	O	L	D	E	R	I	N	G	6 R	7 C
			I		L				C		G	8 C	E	A
			M		I				T		9 E	R	E	C	T	E	D
			U		D				U		R		N		A		E
			L					10 M		M		N		T		L		N
			T			11 M		E				A		R		I		C
	12 P	R	A	T	F	A	L	L		13 I		U		I		A		E
	E		N			N		A		N		T		F		T		D
	D		E		14 L	I	M	N	E	D				U		I		
	A		O			F		C		E				G		O		
	N		U			E		H		C				E		N		
	T		S			S	15 O	D	I	O	U	S			16 P			
	S		L			T		L		S					Y			
			Y			E		Y		I					R			
						D		17 V	E	R	B	I	A	G	E			
								E										

Across
1. The study of the dynamics of projectiles
5. Burning with little smoke and no flame
9. Set up; established
12. Humiliating failure; a fall on the buttocks
14. Described
15. Arousing strong dislike or displeasure
17. Wordiness

Down
2. Having or revealing little emotion
3. Overwhelming, advancing sight crushing all in its path
4. Authoritative pronouncement
5. Happening at the same time
6. Returning like for like, especially evil
7. With a rhythmic flow
8. Apparatus consisting of a compartment spun around a central axis
10. Sadness; gloominess
11. Showed; revealed
12. Those who flaunt their knowledge
13. Not able to make a decision
16. A pile of combustible materials for burning a corpse

Fahrenheit 451 Vocabulary Juggle Letters 1

1. SQOTERGUE = 1. _____
   Bizarre; distorted

2. ORACANDM = 2. _____
   Indian Spice

3. ITLODS = 3. _____
   Having or revealing little emotion

4. IELNDM = 4. _____
   Described

5. UUJEGGNTRA = 5. _____
   Overwhelming, advancing sight crushing all in its path

6. RDEIRPA = 6. _____
   Deflected; avoided

7. TPAEDSN = 7. _____
   Those who flaunt their knowledge

8. LEYMOCLNHA = 8. _____
   Sadness; gloominess

9. CTDEREE = 9. _____
   Set up; established

10. ROCAEWCID = 10. _____
    Lacks courage in the face of danger

11. RPYE = 11. _____
    A pile of combustible materials for burning a corpse

12. OMUBCSELTOINNB = 12. _____
    Does not burn easily

13. TATICLDEEFMU = 13. _____
    Having many faces

14. BPCIYPMILTREE = 14. _____
    Impossible to detect by ordinary senses

15. IODOUS = 15. _____
    Arousing strong dislike or displeasure

Fahrenheit 451 Vocabulary Juggle Letters 1 Answer Key

1. SQOTERGUE = 1. GROTESQUE
   Bizarre; distorted

2. ORACANDM = 2. CARDAMON
   Indian Spice

3. ITLODS = 3. STOLID
   Having or revealing little emotion

4. IELNDM = 4. LIMNED
   Described

5. UUJEGGNTRA = 5. JUGGERNAUT
   Overwhelming, advancing sight crushing all in its path

6. RDEIRPA = 6. PARRIED
   Deflected; avoided

7. TPAEDSN = 7. PEDANTS
   Those who flaunt their knowledge

8. LEYMOCLNHA = 8. MELANCHOLY
   Sadness; gloominess

9. CTDEREE = 9. ERECTED
   Set up; established

10. ROCAEWCID = 10. COWARDICE
    Lacks courage in the face of danger

11. RPYE = 11. PYRE
    A pile of combustible materials for burning a corpse

12. OMUBCSELTOINNB = 12. NONCOMBUSTIBLE
    Does not burn easily

13. TATICLDEEFMU = 13. MULTIFACETED
    Having many faces

14. BPCIYPMILTREE = 14. IMPERCEPTIBLY
    Impossible to detect by ordinary senses

15. IODOUS = 15. ODIOUS
    Arousing strong dislike or displeasure

Fahrenheit 451 Vocabulary Juggle Letters 2

1. LATCETI = 1. _____
   Relating to the sense of touch

2. TIDSLO = 2. _____
   Having or revealing little emotion

3. CTOESOBBNUMLNI = 3. _____
   Does not burn easily

4. ETEPLCPIRIYBM = 4. _____
   Impossible to detect by ordinary senses

5. NADSTPE = 5. _____
   Those who flaunt their knowledge

6. ERLPCCAETE = 6. _____
   A container that holds matter

7. TAFLPLAR = 7. _____
   Humiliating failure; a fall on the buttocks

8. YLEHOAMCNL = 8. _____
   Sadness; gloominess

9. EDRECET = 9. _____
   Set up; established

10. FTLDCTUEEAIM =10. _____
    Having many faces

11. RELIDUZEPV =11. _____
    Reduced to powder

12. ANDEDCCE =12. _____
    With a rhythmic flow

13. RYEP =13. _____
    A pile of combustible materials for burning a corpse

14. UORASENV =14. _____
    Extremely hungry; greedy for gratification

15. UTEECGRNIF =15. _____
    Apparatus consisting of a compartment spun around a central axis

Fahrenheit 451 Vocabulary Juggle Letters 2 Answer Key

1. LATCETI = 1. TACTILE
   Relating to the sense of touch

2. TIDSLO = 2. STOLID
   Having or revealing little emotion

3. CTOESOBBNUMLNI = 3. NONCOMBUSTIBLE
   Does not burn easily

4. ETEPLCPIRIYBM = 4. IMPERCEPTIBLY
   Impossible to detect by ordinary senses

5. NADSTPE = 5. PEDANTS
   Those who flaunt their knowledge

6. ERLPCCAETE = 6. RECEPTACLE
   A container that holds matter

7. TAFLPLAR = 7. PRATFALL
   Humiliating failure; a fall on the buttocks

8. YLEHOAMCNL = 8. MELANCHOLY
   Sadness; gloominess

9. EDRECET = 9. ERECTED
   Set up; established

10. FTLDCTUEEAIM = 10. MULTIFACETED
    Having many faces

11. RELIDUZEPV = 11. PULVERIZED
    Reduced to powder

12. ANDEDCCE = 12. CADENCED
    With a rhythmic flow

13. RYEP = 13. PYRE
    A pile of combustible materials for burning a corpse

14. UORASENV = 14. RAVENOUS
    Extremely hungry; greedy for gratification

15. UTEECGRNIF = 15. CENTRIFUGE
    Apparatus consisting of a compartment spun around a central axis

Fahrenheit 451 Vocabulary Juggle Letters 3

1. EDADCNEC = 1. _____
With a rhythmic flow

2. SOIDUO = 2. _____
Arousing strong dislike or displeasure

3. ERBAVIEG = 3. _____
Wordiness

4. ORDLGSENIM = 4. _____
Burning with little smoke and no flame

5. ENTDPAS = 5. _____
Those who flaunt their knowledge

6. MATIUSELOYLSUN = 6. _____
Happening at the same time

7. ALARPYCIL = 7. _____
Fine; small in diameter

8. IWEROACDC = 8. _____
Lacks courage in the face of danger

9. REPY = 9. _____
A pile of combustible materials for burning a corpse

10. LACLMOEYHN = 10. _____
Sadness; gloominess

11. LECAETEPCR = 11. _____
A container that holds matter

12. OAILATIRTNE = 12. _____
Returning like for like, especially evil

13. UVASERON = 13. _____
Extremely hungry; greedy for gratification

14. TCEUNEGIFR = 14. _____
Apparatus consisting of a compartment spun around a central axis

15. DECERTE = 15. _____
Set up; established

Fahrenheit 451 Vocabulary Juggle Letters 3 Answer Key

1. EDADCNEC = 1. CADENCED
   With a rhythmic flow

2. SOIDUO = 2. ODIOUS
   Arousing strong dislike or displeasure

3. ERBAVIEG = 3. VERBIAGE
   Wordiness

4. ORDLGSENIM = 4. SMOLDERING
   Burning with little smoke and no flame

5. ENTDPAS = 5. PEDANTS
   Those who flaunt their knowledge

6. MATIUSELOYLSUN = 6. SIMULTANEOUSLY
   Happening at the same time

7. ALARPYCIL = 7. CAPILLARY
   Fine; small in diameter

8. IWEROACDC = 8. COWARDICE
   Lacks courage in the face of danger

9. REPY = 9. PYRE
   A pile of combustible materials for burning a corpse

10. LACLMOEYHN = 10. MELANCHOLY
    Sadness; gloominess

11. LECAETEPCR = 11. RECEPTACLE
    A container that holds matter

12. OAILATIRTNE = 12. RETALIATION
    Returning like for like, especially evil

13. UVASERON = 13. RAVENOUS
    Extremely hungry; greedy for gratification

14. TCEUNEGIFR = 14. CENTRIFUGE
    Apparatus consisting of a compartment spun around a central axis

15. DECERTE = 15. ERECTED
    Set up; established

Fahrenheit 451 Vocabulary Juggle Letters 4

1. RUESBOC = 1. _____
Not readily noticed or seen; not commonly known

2. APNSTED = 2. _____
Those who flaunt their knowledge

3. AHOCNLLEMY = 3. _____
Sadness; gloominess

4. IVNIIDECES = 4. _____
Not able to make a decision

5. TSEIRCLIIVOP = 5. _____
Predispositions; tendencies

6. TASISILBLC = 6. _____
The study of the dynamics of projectiles

7. UCTMID = 7. _____
Authoritative pronouncement

8. EAIBVGRE = 8. _____
Wordiness

9. EOTALTINRAI = 9. _____
Returning like for like, especially evil

10. DCRMNAAO = 10. _____
Indian Spice

11. ENCDACDE = 11. _____
With a rhythmic flow

12. TSODLI = 12. _____
Having or revealing little emotion

13. IETCTLA = 13. _____
Relating to the sense of touch

14. MUTOBOSIELCNBN = 14. _____
Does not burn easily

15. EAFEDMISNT = 15. _____
Showed; revealed

Fahrenheit 451 Vocabulary Juggle Letters 4 Answer Key

1. RUESBOC = 1. OBSCURE
Not readily noticed or seen; not commonly known

2. APNSTED = 2. PEDANTS
Those who flaunt their knowledge

3. AHOCNLLEMY = 3. MELANCHOLY
Sadness; gloominess

4. IVNIIDECES = 4. INDECISIVE
Not able to make a decision

5. TSEIRCLIIVOP = 5. PROCLIVITIES
Predispositions; tendencies

6. TASISILBLC = 6. BALLISTICS
The study of the dynamics of projectiles

7. UCTMID = 7. DICTUM
Authoritative pronouncement

8. EAIBVGRE = 8. VERBIAGE
Wordiness

9. EOTALTINRAI = 9. RETALIATION
Returning like for like, especially evil

10. DCRMNAAO = 10. CARDAMON
Indian Spice

11. ENCDACDE = 11. CADENCED
With a rhythmic flow

12. TSODLI = 12. STOLID
Having or revealing little emotion

13. IETCTLA = 13. TACTILE
Relating to the sense of touch

14. MUTOBOSIELCNBN = 14. NONCOMBUSTIBLE
Does not burn easily

15. EAFEDMISNT = 15. MANIFESTED
Showed; revealed

BALLISTICS	The study of the dynamics of projectiles
CADENCED	With a rhythmic flow
CAPILLARY	Fine; small in diameter
CARDAMON	Indian Spice
CENTRIFUGE	Apparatus consisting of a compartment spun around a central axis
COWARDICE	Lacks courage in the face of danger

DICTUM	Authoritative pronouncement
ERECTED	Set up; established
GROTESQUE	Bizarre; distorted
IMPERCEPTIBLY	Impossible to detect by ordinary senses
INDECISIVE	Not able to make a decision
JUGGERNAUT	Overwhelming, advancing sight crushing all in its path

LIMNED	Described
MANIFESTED	Showed; revealed
MELANCHOLY	Sadness; gloominess
MULTIFACETED	Having many faces
NONCOMBUSTIBLE	Does not burn easily
OBSCURE	Not readily noticed or seen; not commonly known

ODIOUS	Arousing strong dislike or displeasure
PARRIED	Deflected; avoided
PEDANTS	Those who flaunt their knowledge
PRATFALL	Humiliating failure; a fall on the buttocks
PROCLIVITIES	Predispositions; tendencies
PULVERIZED	Reduced to powder

PYRE	A pile of combustible materials for burning a corpse
RAVENOUS	Extremely hungry; greedy for gratification
RECEPTACLE	A container that holds matter
REFRACTED	Deflected from a straight path
RETALIATION	Returning like for like, especially evil
SIMULTANEOUSLY	Happening at the same time

SMOLDERING	Burning with little smoke and no flame
STOLID	Having or revealing little emotion
TACTILE	Relating to the sense of touch
VERBIAGE	Wordiness

Fahrenheit 451 Vocabulary

INDECISIVE	PYRE	SIMULTANEOUSLY	RECEPTACLE	ERECTED
MANIFESTED	PULVERIZED	COWARDICE	BALLISTICS	CARDAMON
NONCOMBUSTIBLE	SMOLDERING	FREE SPACE	OBSCURE	JUGGERNAUT
DICTUM	ODIOUS	STOLID	VERBIAGE	MULTIFACETED
CENTRIFUGE	LIMNED	IMPERCEPTIBLY	CAPILLARY	RETALIATION

Fahrenheit 451 Vocabulary

PROCLIVITIES	GROTESQUE	PEDANTS	PARRIED	CADENCED
RAVENOUS	PRATFALL	TACTILE	REFRACTED	RETALIATION
CAPILLARY	IMPERCEPTIBLY	FREE SPACE	CENTRIFUGE	MULTIFACETED
VERBIAGE	STOLID	ODIOUS	DICTUM	JUGGERNAUT
OBSCURE	MELANCHOLY	SMOLDERING	NONCOMBUSTIBLE	CARDAMON

Fahrenheit 451 Vocabulary

BALLISTICS	CENTRIFUGE	PYRE	CAPILLARY	REFRACTED
PROCLIVITIES	PEDANTS	STOLID	GROTESQUE	RAVENOUS
RECEPTACLE	ERECTED	FREE SPACE	PULVERIZED	SMOLDERING
SIMULTANEOUSLY	CADENCED	LIMNED	IMPERCEPTIBLY	DICTUM
TACTILE	NONCOMBUSTIBLE	JUGGERNAUT	INDECISIVE	CARDAMON

Fahrenheit 451 Vocabulary

PRATFALL	COWARDICE	PARRIED	MANIFESTED	MULTIFACETED
VERBIAGE	OBSCURE	ODIOUS	RETALIATION	CARDAMON
INDECISIVE	JUGGERNAUT	FREE SPACE	TACTILE	DICTUM
IMPERCEPTIBLY	LIMNED	CADENCED	SIMULTANEOUSLY	SMOLDERING
PULVERIZED	MELANCHOLY	ERECTED	RECEPTACLE	RAVENOUS

Fahrenheit 451 Vocabulary

CAPILLARY	CARDAMON	INDECISIVE	MANIFESTED	STOLID
LIMNED	RECEPTACLE	DICTUM	PRATFALL	PULVERIZED
TACTILE	REFRACTED	FREE SPACE	GROTESQUE	COWARDICE
PROCLIVITIES	JUGGERNAUT	VERBIAGE	CADENCED	MELANCHOLY
PEDANTS	RAVENOUS	BALLISTICS	ERECTED	NONCOMBUSTIBLE

Fahrenheit 451 Vocabulary

CENTRIFUGE	OBSCURE	SMOLDERING	PARRIED	RETALIATION
MULTIFACETED	PYRE	SIMULTANEOUSLY	ODIOUS	NONCOMBUSTIBLE
ERECTED	BALLISTICS	FREE SPACE	PEDANTS	MELANCHOLY
CADENCED	VERBIAGE	JUGGERNAUT	PROCLIVITIES	COWARDICE
GROTESQUE	IMPERCEPTIBLY	REFRACTED	TACTILE	PULVERIZED

Fahrenheit 451 Vocabulary

PARRIED	ODIOUS	PROCLIVITIES	JUGGERNAUT	ERECTED
RECEPTACLE	CADENCED	VERBIAGE	RAVENOUS	INDECISIVE
BALLISTICS	MELANCHOLY	FREE SPACE	OBSCURE	IMPERCEPTIBLY
STOLID	RETALIATION	PULVERIZED	LIMNED	GROTESQUE
PYRE	MANIFESTED	PRATFALL	COWARDICE	CARDAMON

Fahrenheit 451 Vocabulary

PEDANTS	MULTIFACETED	SMOLDERING	TACTILE	SIMULTANEOUSLY
REFRACTED	NONCOMBUSTIBLE	CAPILLARY	CENTRIFUGE	CARDAMON
COWARDICE	PRATFALL	FREE SPACE	PYRE	GROTESQUE
LIMNED	PULVERIZED	RETALIATION	STOLID	IMPERCEPTIBLY
OBSCURE	DICTUM	MELANCHOLY	BALLISTICS	INDECISIVE

Fahrenheit 451 Vocabulary

INDECISIVE	ERECTED	RECEPTACLE	REFRACTED	DICTUM
CAPILLARY	BALLISTICS	PRATFALL	PYRE	JUGGERNAUT
MULTIFACETED	COWARDICE	FREE SPACE	PEDANTS	CENTRIFUGE
OBSCURE	IMPERCEPTIBLY	TACTILE	SMOLDERING	STOLID
MANIFESTED	VERBIAGE	RETALIATION	GROTESQUE	RAVENOUS

Fahrenheit 451 Vocabulary

PARRIED	CADENCED	LIMNED	PROCLIVITIES	PULVERIZED
ODIOUS	MELANCHOLY	SIMULTANEOUSLY	NONCOMBUSTIBLE	RAVENOUS
GROTESQUE	RETALIATION	FREE SPACE	MANIFESTED	STOLID
SMOLDERING	TACTILE	IMPERCEPTIBLY	OBSCURE	CENTRIFUGE
PEDANTS	CARDAMON	COWARDICE	MULTIFACETED	JUGGERNAUT

Fahrenheit 451 Vocabulary

CAPILLARY	OBSCURE	COWARDICE	ODIOUS	MULTIFACETED
RETALIATION	SMOLDERING	PYRE	STOLID	INDECISIVE
PRATFALL	TACTILE	FREE SPACE	PULVERIZED	RAVENOUS
CENTRIFUGE	NONCOMBUSTIBLE	VERBIAGE	LIMNED	DICTUM
JUGGERNAUT	BALLISTICS	PEDANTS	RECEPTACLE	REFRACTED

Fahrenheit 451 Vocabulary

PROCLIVITIES	MANIFESTED	CADENCED	IMPERCEPTIBLY	PARRIED
ERECTED	GROTESQUE	SIMULTANEOUSLY	MELANCHOLY	REFRACTED
RECEPTACLE	PEDANTS	FREE SPACE	JUGGERNAUT	DICTUM
LIMNED	VERBIAGE	NONCOMBUSTIBLE	CENTRIFUGE	RAVENOUS
PULVERIZED	CARDAMON	TACTILE	PRATFALL	INDECISIVE

Fahrenheit 451 Vocabulary

PULVERIZED	ODIOUS	ERECTED	IMPERCEPTIBLY	PYRE
NONCOMBUSTIBLE	GROTESQUE	PARRIED	RAVENOUS	TACTILE
OBSCURE	MULTIFACETED	FREE SPACE	COWARDICE	LIMNED
CENTRIFUGE	DICTUM	PROCLIVITIES	CAPILLARY	INDECISIVE
CADENCED	SIMULTANEOUSLY	JUGGERNAUT	RETALIATION	REFRACTED

Fahrenheit 451 Vocabulary

RECEPTACLE	CARDAMON	SMOLDERING	BALLISTICS	PRATFALL
VERBIAGE	MELANCHOLY	STOLID	MANIFESTED	REFRACTED
RETALIATION	JUGGERNAUT	FREE SPACE	CADENCED	INDECISIVE
CAPILLARY	PROCLIVITIES	DICTUM	CENTRIFUGE	LIMNED
COWARDICE	PEDANTS	MULTIFACETED	OBSCURE	TACTILE

Fahrenheit 451 Vocabulary

NONCOMBUSTIBLE	PRATFALL	OBSCURE	ERECTED	PROCLIVITIES
MANIFESTED	PYRE	IMPERCEPTIBLY	RETALIATION	DICTUM
BALLISTICS	PULVERIZED	FREE SPACE	LIMNED	SIMULTANEOUSLY
RECEPTACLE	TACTILE	PEDANTS	STOLID	PARRIED
ODIOUS	INDECISIVE	RAVENOUS	GROTESQUE	MELANCHOLY

Fahrenheit 451 Vocabulary

VERBIAGE	CAPILLARY	MULTIFACETED	CARDAMON	JUGGERNAUT
CADENCED	SMOLDERING	REFRACTED	CENTRIFUGE	MELANCHOLY
GROTESQUE	RAVENOUS	FREE SPACE	ODIOUS	PARRIED
STOLID	PEDANTS	TACTILE	RECEPTACLE	SIMULTANEOUSLY
LIMNED	COWARDICE	PULVERIZED	BALLISTICS	DICTUM

Fahrenheit 451 Vocabulary

MULTIFACETED	MELANCHOLY	JUGGERNAUT	NONCOMBUSTIBLE	INDECISIVE
RAVENOUS	MANIFESTED	PYRE	PULVERIZED	PARRIED
COWARDICE	PEDANTS	FREE SPACE	SIMULTANEOUSLY	LIMNED
RECEPTACLE	REFRACTED	RETALIATION	VERBIAGE	CAPILLARY
OBSCURE	ERECTED	PRATFALL	ODIOUS	STOLID

Fahrenheit 451 Vocabulary

TACTILE	BALLISTICS	PROCLIVITIES	CARDAMON	DICTUM
CENTRIFUGE	CADENCED	IMPERCEPTIBLY	GROTESQUE	STOLID
ODIOUS	PRATFALL	FREE SPACE	OBSCURE	CAPILLARY
VERBIAGE	RETALIATION	REFRACTED	RECEPTACLE	LIMNED
SIMULTANEOUSLY	SMOLDERING	PEDANTS	COWARDICE	PARRIED

Fahrenheit 451 Vocabulary

RECEPTACLE	VERBIAGE	REFRACTED	TACTILE	OBSCURE
CENTRIFUGE	CARDAMON	PYRE	IMPERCEPTIBLY	MELANCHOLY
PROCLIVITIES	MANIFESTED	FREE SPACE	JUGGERNAUT	NONCOMBUSTIBLE
PULVERIZED	RETALIATION	SMOLDERING	CADENCED	PRATFALL
BALLISTICS	PEDANTS	ERECTED	SIMULTANEOUSLY	INDECISIVE

Fahrenheit 451 Vocabulary

PARRIED	CAPILLARY	ODIOUS	MULTIFACETED	DICTUM
STOLID	RAVENOUS	LIMNED	GROTESQUE	INDECISIVE
SIMULTANEOUSLY	ERECTED	FREE SPACE	BALLISTICS	PRATFALL
CADENCED	SMOLDERING	RETALIATION	PULVERIZED	NONCOMBUSTIBLE
JUGGERNAUT	COWARDICE	MANIFESTED	PROCLIVITIES	MELANCHOLY

Fahrenheit 451 Vocabulary

RAVENOUS	RECEPTACLE	TACTILE	CADENCED	CAPILLARY
RETALIATION	NONCOMBUSTIBLE	PROCLIVITIES	OBSCURE	REFRACTED
ODIOUS	PYRE	FREE SPACE	JUGGERNAUT	ERECTED
VERBIAGE	PULVERIZED	SIMULTANEOUSLY	CENTRIFUGE	DICTUM
STOLID	BALLISTICS	MANIFESTED	MULTIFACETED	INDECISIVE

Fahrenheit 451 Vocabulary

CARDAMON	PRATFALL	IMPERCEPTIBLY	SMOLDERING	LIMNED
MELANCHOLY	PARRIED	COWARDICE	GROTESQUE	INDECISIVE
MULTIFACETED	MANIFESTED	FREE SPACE	STOLID	DICTUM
CENTRIFUGE	SIMULTANEOUSLY	PULVERIZED	VERBIAGE	ERECTED
JUGGERNAUT	PEDANTS	PYRE	ODIOUS	REFRACTED

Fahrenheit 451 Vocabulary

NONCOMBUSTIBLE	ERECTED	CAPILLARY	PARRIED	MULTIFACETED
RETALIATION	DICTUM	INDECISIVE	CENTRIFUGE	CADENCED
SIMULTANEOUSLY	STOLID	FREE SPACE	SMOLDERING	GROTESQUE
LIMNED	TACTILE	MANIFESTED	PRATFALL	RAVENOUS
ODIOUS	PEDANTS	MELANCHOLY	CARDAMON	PYRE

Fahrenheit 451 Vocabulary

PULVERIZED	RECEPTACLE	PROCLIVITIES	VERBIAGE	OBSCURE
REFRACTED	BALLISTICS	JUGGERNAUT	IMPERCEPTIBLY	PYRE
CARDAMON	MELANCHOLY	FREE SPACE	ODIOUS	RAVENOUS
PRATFALL	MANIFESTED	TACTILE	LIMNED	GROTESQUE
SMOLDERING	COWARDICE	STOLID	SIMULTANEOUSLY	CADENCED

Fahrenheit 451 Vocabulary

COWARDICE	PEDANTS	ERECTED	JUGGERNAUT	PARRIED
PRATFALL	STOLID	LIMNED	RAVENOUS	MANIFESTED
CAPILLARY	MULTIFACETED	FREE SPACE	OBSCURE	TACTILE
PULVERIZED	SMOLDERING	BALLISTICS	MELANCHOLY	GROTESQUE
PROCLIVITIES	INDECISIVE	PYRE	IMPERCEPTIBLY	SIMULTANEOUSLY

Fahrenheit 451 Vocabulary

REFRACTED	CARDAMON	RETALIATION	NONCOMBUSTIBLE	DICTUM
RECEPTACLE	VERBIAGE	CADENCED	ODIOUS	SIMULTANEOUSLY
IMPERCEPTIBLY	PYRE	FREE SPACE	PROCLIVITIES	GROTESQUE
MELANCHOLY	BALLISTICS	SMOLDERING	PULVERIZED	TACTILE
OBSCURE	CENTRIFUGE	MULTIFACETED	CAPILLARY	MANIFESTED

Fahrenheit 451 Vocabulary

ERECTED	PYRE	STOLID	RAVENOUS	SMOLDERING
PULVERIZED	CADENCED	IMPERCEPTIBLY	CARDAMON	PROCLIVITIES
OBSCURE	RETALIATION	FREE SPACE	CENTRIFUGE	JUGGERNAUT
CAPILLARY	RECEPTACLE	ODIOUS	PRATFALL	GROTESQUE
NONCOMBUSTIBLE	PEDANTS	INDECISIVE	MANIFESTED	MELANCHOLY

Fahrenheit 451 Vocabulary

REFRACTED	MULTIFACETED	LIMNED	COWARDICE	VERBIAGE
SIMULTANEOUSLY	BALLISTICS	DICTUM	PARRIED	MELANCHOLY
MANIFESTED	INDECISIVE	FREE SPACE	NONCOMBUSTIBLE	GROTESQUE
PRATFALL	ODIOUS	RECEPTACLE	CAPILLARY	JUGGERNAUT
CENTRIFUGE	TACTILE	RETALIATION	OBSCURE	PROCLIVITIES

Fahrenheit 451 Vocabulary

PEDANTS	PRATFALL	CENTRIFUGE	REFRACTED	CADENCED
ODIOUS	SIMULTANEOUSLY	MULTIFACETED	TACTILE	DICTUM
PULVERIZED	NONCOMBUSTIBLE	FREE SPACE	RAVENOUS	MELANCHOLY
GROTESQUE	RETALIATION	CARDAMON	JUGGERNAUT	IMPERCEPTIBLY
RECEPTACLE	SMOLDERING	PYRE	BALLISTICS	ERECTED

Fahrenheit 451 Vocabulary

MANIFESTED	PARRIED	COWARDICE	OBSCURE	LIMNED
VERBIAGE	INDECISIVE	CAPILLARY	PROCLIVITIES	ERECTED
BALLISTICS	PYRE	FREE SPACE	RECEPTACLE	IMPERCEPTIBLY
JUGGERNAUT	CARDAMON	RETALIATION	GROTESQUE	MELANCHOLY
RAVENOUS	STOLID	NONCOMBUSTIBLE	PULVERIZED	DICTUM

Fahrenheit 451 Vocabulary

VERBIAGE	NONCOMBUSTIBLE	MELANCHOLY	SMOLDERING	MANIFESTED
DICTUM	CAPILLARY	ERECTED	MULTIFACETED	RECEPTACLE
PULVERIZED	SIMULTANEOUSLY	FREE SPACE	RAVENOUS	GROTESQUE
PYRE	PRATFALL	JUGGERNAUT	RETALIATION	REFRACTED
PROCLIVITIES	CADENCED	CARDAMON	COWARDICE	PARRIED

Fahrenheit 451 Vocabulary

TACTILE	INDECISIVE	CENTRIFUGE	STOLID	PEDANTS
LIMNED	BALLISTICS	IMPERCEPTIBLY	OBSCURE	PARRIED
COWARDICE	CARDAMON	FREE SPACE	PROCLIVITIES	REFRACTED
RETALIATION	JUGGERNAUT	PRATFALL	PYRE	GROTESQUE
RAVENOUS	ODIOUS	SIMULTANEOUSLY	PULVERIZED	RECEPTACLE

www.ingramcontent.com/pod-product-compliance
Lightning Source LLC
LaVergne TN
LVHW081538060526
838200LV00048B/2132